The Family Piano Doctor

The Family Piano Doctor

A step-by-step guide to the
repairing, tuning and renovating
of the family piano

Don Wicks

B.T. Batsford Limited · London

ISBN 0 7134 6732 0

Typeset by Servis Filmsetting Ltd, Manchester

and printed in Great Britain by The Bath Press, Avon

for the Publisher
B.T. Batsford Ltd
4 Fitzhardinge Street
London W1H 0AH

A catalogue entry on this title is
available from the British Library

Contents

726070

Acknowledgements

Many thanks to:
Andrew, my son, for the photography and the encouragement; Margaret, my wife, for remaining in regular, full-time employment; Gaynor 'Miss Pringle from the Agency' Lewis, for her support; Ron Lawrence, for providing the drawings; Derek Lewis, for his photographic processing services; and my editors at Batsford, Tim Auger and Liz Radford, for their sound advice during the various stages of production.

Introduction

In this age of D.I.Y. the average person seems to be capable of repairing just about everything around the house—except the piano. Mysteries surround the piano tuner, particularly when he is involved with, say the 'tempering of intervals', and the onlooker cannot ever see himself being capable of such an elusive art, knowing that the professional tuner has spent many years of concentrated study in order to have acquired such skills. However, any person of average intelligence should be able to make a reasonable job of tuning and repairing the family piano, though it must be understood that the advice and instructions contained in the following pages are not enough for the reader to set him or herself up as a professional piano tuner and repairer.

This book is about giving new life to an ageing, dying piano and deals with such frustrating problems as broken action parts, sticking keys and unwanted noises; the correction of these problems being within the abilities of the average person. Major structural repairs, such as fitting new tuning planks and sound-boards are not dealt with here, as these areas of repair are best left to those with specialist knowledge and equipment.

Piano tuners and repairers are in short supply and it can be difficult to gain their services. Repairs can be expensive, usually because of the labour costs involved, and in many instances a technician may not be prepared to work on a battered, tired, old piano.

This is where you come in. All you need is normal eyesight and hearing, a steady hand, and . . . lots of patience!

If you do not already own a piano but wish to buy one and know little or nothing about them, then reading through this book will give you an insight into what to look out for. If you already have a piano and have carried out some of the repairs as described in the following chapters, then this book will increase your knowledge of the business should you wish to acquire a better quality piano. A guide to what to look for when buying a used piano is given below.

ACTION AND STRINGS

A piano can be either vertically strung, i.e. all the strings falling parallel to each other from top to bottom, or overstrung, i.e. the copper-wound bass strings crossing diagonally over the all-steel treble strings. The overstrung design is far superior, since strings fitted diagonally have a greater length in a given area, and more strings cross the sensitive central regions of the soundboard, creating a fuller sound.

An underdamped action, the usual arrangement seen in an overstrung, upright piano is to be preferred to an overdamped system. Underdamping is more effective because the felts operate nearer the centres of the strings, and thus stop the vibration of the strings more quickly than if they were nearer the ends.

Obvious defects in action and strings are usually less serious than hidden defects. A broken hammer or two, or a few missing strings, within reason, are not expensive to repair or replace and these matters are dealt with later in the book. The most serious defect, and it usually cannot be seen, is a cracked or dried-out tuning plank, this plank being the board that receives the tuning pins. If the pins do not fit tightly into the plank then the piano may be quite untunable, or at best, will not stand in tune for long. The cost of fitting a new plank is prohibitive and is only warranted in good quality pianos. Thanks to modern central-heating systems, dried-out planks are more common now than they ever were, and not only in old pianos. You should suspect loose tuning-pins when a piano is so ridiculously out of tune that when one key is played it sounds like two. Although loose tuning-pins are dealt with later in this book, I would not advise that you buy a piano knowing, or suspecting, that this defect exists.

KEYBOARD

Missing or damaged white key coverings are easily replaceable and inexpensive. Sticking keys are very common in second-hand pianos, particularly if the piano has been in a damp atmosphere, or rarely played. If the problem lies within the keys then it can be dealt with easily, but if it is caused by the action then there may be a more serious defect. To check this, use the tip of your finger to flick the action from underneath, as if being activated by the key; if the system works and returns rapidly to rest then it is the key itself which is at fault.

SOUNDBOARD

Cracks in a soundboard can sometimes be seen but if situated behind a section of the iron frame then they may be hidden from view. A tell-tale sign of cracks is that strings sounding in the region where cracks appear produce a dull thud rather than a ringing tone. Soundboard damage can be expensive to repair.

One defect in the soundboard which cannot be seen is 'crown loss'. A soundboard is manufactured to bow out against, and resist, the pressure of the strings. The curvature is very slight, but over many years, and quite invisibly to the naked eye, the soundboard gradually flattens out due to the constant and enormous downward pressure of the strings, the tone quality deteriorating simultaneously and eventually disappearing altogether. This condition is beyond repair, and although the resulting 'saloon-bar' sound may be quite amusing when playing 'silent movie' type themes, it is of little use for general study.

FRAME

The wooden frame went out of production before the end of the nineteenth century; it is rarely seen nowadays and is not a recommended buy. Cracks in iron frames only appear once in several thousand but those pianos with cracked frames are rendered worthless. The middle octaves of a piano, even on a neglected instrument, should be comparable with the range of the human singing voice, and a reasonable rise in pitch, note by note, from bass to treble should be evident. Should these conditions not exist, be suspicious. Remove the action (described later) and, using a torch if necessary, examine the frame thoroughly.

CASEWORK

A piano is firstly a musical instrument and secondly a piece of furniture. A fine sounding instrument, in a good state of mechanical repair, is a musical instrument, whatever its appearance. A piano with an attractive, unblemished casework, but with an unexciting sound and many mechanical defects is a lesser instrument, if a musical instrument at all. An upright piano which has had its casework modernized may be much older than its appearance may suggest. Some tell-tale signs:

1. Two names, one proudly cast into the iron frame and another in gold transfer lettering on the fallboard (lid).

2.   A modern type music shelf on the fallboard, yet with rebates (grooves) still apparent at the top of the front panel where a folding shelf of the older type was once fitted.

3.   Panels and other wooden parts of more than one grain and colour.

4.   A lack of uniformity in the apparent age of different parts, for example, a 'newish' look about the action, particularly the bridle tapes (explained later), yet well-worn black and white keys.

5.   Slight traces of gold paint on the strings near the tuning pins which indicate that the plank or frame may have been brightened up.

WOODWORM

Check for pin holes and a collection of white dust, often seen in the keys and on the keybed (removing the keys and exposing the keybed is explained later). Do not buy a piano if this condition is evident because, if still active, woodworm can affect other parts of the piano as well as furniture in the household. Should it be your misfortune to have a piano with such a problem then proprietary brands of woodworm killer are readily obtainable. Clean away the dust and apply the solution as instructed by the manufacturers. Monitor the situation and if the dust re-appears then the best advice is that you arrange for the piano to be incinerated.

ANTIQUE VALUE

Outside the very small specialized group of people who collect such things an old piano has no antique value. Unlike violins and good wine, a piano does not improve as it ages, but gradually deteriorates until it becomes useless, although with careful looking after a piano can last a hundred years or more from new.

PITCH

If the piano to be purchased is to be played with another instrument (this includes the voice), then the pitch should be considered. Old pianos, of not too robust a construction, with evidence of rust on the strings and already well under pitch, may be incapable of being brought up to standard pitch. It is advisable to compare the piano's pitch with its partner instrument, or to check it with a tuning fork.

PREVENTATIVE MAINTENANCE

Precautions can be taken to reduce the risk of serious defects occurring in your piano. A piano should never be placed near a radiator, exposed to excessive heat or to direct sunlight, as such conditions can lead to tuning plank, soundboard and casework problems.

Steamy and damp atmospheres should also be avoided, as these can result in sticking or 'slow' keys and action parts, as well as causing rust on metal parts. Proprietary brands of humidifiers for dry conditions, and heating lamps for cold, damp conditions, may help if ideal circumstances are not possible.

A WORD ABOUT GRAND PIANOS

Should you own a grand piano and would like to do your own tuning and repairs then most of what follows concerning the care and repair of upright pianos also applies to grands. Before carrying out any task on your grand refer to the earlier related section for the upright, as well as reading the appropriate notes specifically relating to the grand.

Perhaps the most valuable advice that can be given when about to work on a grand is that you should not be awed or intimidated by the size of this noble beast. The horizontal body structure, long legs and the lid which opens to the sky accentuate its might, but if bundled together into a compact package then a small grand is no bigger than a large upright.

The horizontal string design must be seen as a benefit, as it allows the law of gravity to assist in some of the action movements. The dampers, for example, fall back under their own weight and the system is of a straightforward design. The hammer return is also gravity-assisted, eliminating the need for bridle tapes.

Generally, repairing and tuning a grand is no more difficult than performing the same tasks on an upright and to know this will help you to accept the challenge with a relaxed state of mind.

Cleaning

UPRIGHT PIANOS

Taking a piano apart, giving it a much-needed spring-clean, and putting it back together again is not the formidable task that many people think it is. Use your common sense and the job is as good as done. Give yourself plenty of room to work in and arrange for a table, long enough to take the action, to be close by.

Remove the top and bottom panels and the fallboard. The action can now be seen. Usually, actions in overstrung, under-damped pianos have metal standards (the stands at each end), and are locked into position with nuts. The actions in vertical, overdamped pianos have wooden standards and are held in position with catches on the sides.

Remove the action and place on a table. An action with metal standards, known as 'having its own feet', will stand comfortably on the table, but to make sure it is not knocked over accidentally, hefty weights, such as cardboard boxes filled with bean tins, should be placed at either side.

Most actions with wooden standards have dowels at the base, so use two short pieces of wood (skirting or facia board would be ideal), each with holes bored large enough to receive the dowels, to ensure that the action does not rock and is kept in a stable position. Any sensible makeshift idea will do, as long as safety precautions are observed. For added security place a weight at either side as described above.

The keys, which are fitted over two pins, can now be removed. Do not use force on any stubborn ones, as they break easily, but, using two hands, one to the front end and one at the back, tease them out gently. To avoid a mix-up (one key will never fit properly into another's place), number the keys from bottom to top, 1–85, and place them safely in order on a table.

Check for large foreign objects around the keybed and underneath, where the pedals are, and remove any you find. This will avoid any damage to the vacuum cleaner used in the next stage of the cleaning operation. Fit a long nozzle attachment to the cleaner and use in conjuction with a medium-size paint brush, using the brush to free caked-up deposits. When cleaning the keybed, make sure that the felt washers around the two rails of key pins do not suddenly disappear into the vacuum cleaner. Clean out the bottom of the piano (often a wildlife sanctuary) where the pedal system is located, again using brush and nozzle.

Wipe all the wooden surfaces with a damp cloth, avoiding contact with felted and metal parts—particularly the strings—and finish off with a dry cloth. The key pins, if rusted, can be cleaned with a cloth and a little light oil, which should then be wiped off immediately.

Old wives' tales abound as to effective methods of cleaning white key tops, such as using milk and even vinegar. I suggest that you use a cloth dipped in a weak solution of washing-up liquid. The rest of the key can be cleaned in this way too, but must then be dried off thoroughly. A light sanding of the bare wooden sides and tops will give that 'as good as new' appearance. Think twice about using sandpaper on the white key tops, because if they are scored this will annoy the person who plays the piano.

When cleaning the action do not dust the hammers from side to side, but stand in front and brush towards you. An artist's brush is useful for getting into awkward corners.

With a slightly damp cloth carefully wipe the hammer tails and backchecks, one at a time and holding them steady, and then do the same to all other wooden parts which are accessible. **Warning:** Never use a powerful airline on a disintegrating piano action or you may never see your action again.

When all is satisfactorily done replace the keys one by one, in order, from bottom to top and lock the action back into the piano.

GRAND PIANOS

There is one particular problem associated with the grand which is not usually encountered with the upright, and that is the removal and replacement of the action. If this task can be performed safely then no special difficulty, either in the cleaning or in the rest of the servicing schedules, should present itself.

First of all, a little explanation. The keys in a grand piano are held in position by a 'keyframe'. The frame has three rails running lengthwise, for the front pins, the balance pins and the backtouch. The rails are stabilized by cross-members. The 'action frame', which holds together all the action parts, is screwed to the keyframe, so to 'take the action out of the piano' includes the removal of the keys. (The action in an upright is not attached to the keys and can be taken out leaving the keys in position.) The base in the main structure of the piano that both the keyframe and action frame sit on is the 'keybed'.

Removing the action

1. Open the top lid, remove the music stand and fallboard.

2. Unscrew the key-stop rail (this runs along the keys behind the black keys).

3. The black keyblocks at each end of the keyboard will be screwed in from underneath the keybed, usually with finger-grip screws. Feel underneath, unscrew and remove the keyblocks.

4. The keyslip can now be taken out. It will be held in place either by dowels, in which case it can be pulled out, or screwed in from underneath. Remove and put to one side.

5. Check the lid drop (the board facing you that the fall rests against when in an open position). This is an important precaution since, if the lid drop is below the level of the iron frame, the hammers may catch on it (when the action is drawn out) and break. Feel with the hand underneath the board and decide whether it is flush with the iron frame, or protrudes below. If it is flush then leave it where it is. If it protrudes below the iron frame it needs to be removed. If it is slotted into place then it can be lifted out easily. If screwed in position, then you will find a few fixing screws in the iron frame near the tuning pins.

6. Look through the strings at the hammers. Should any hammers ride higher than the general level push them into line by inserting a narrow tool through the strings. If a hammer springs back to its original position lower it by adjusting the metal capstan at the end of the key. Using a thin, pointed rod, turn the capstan to the left (clockwise).

7. Place a table or bench at the side of the piano. This must be big and strong enough to receive the action.

8. Make sure the floor space in this area is clear.

That was the easy part—now down to the real business. A grand action is taken out, and put back in again, by feeling, looking and listening. Though heavy (and even more so with outstretched arms), its removal remains a one-man job and you don't want any helpers. Your best ally is a good breakfast.

9. Standing in front of the piano, with outstretched arms, grip the ends of the keyframe.

10. Check that your thumbs do not depress the two end keys.

11. Check that your stomach is not depressing any keys in the middle.

12. Without touching any keys, look through the strings at the hammers and carefully pull the keyframe forward, making a little tug with the left hand, then the right, then the left, etc. Keep checking over the top until the hammers have passed out of sight. If, during these first movements, you touch any of the keys you will be rewarded with the most delightful of sounds as the hammers break, like that of fresh carrots snapping.

13. As the action comes more and more over the keybed there will be a tendency for it to drop at the front end. To counteract this, raise the front end slightly and maintain the low hammer line. Keep tugging, left hand, right hand etc., until the hammers have safely cleared the lid drop and are in full view.

14. Change your grip (but do not let go) to a stronger, central position on the keyframe.

15. Completely remove the action and place on the bench.

An opportunity to investigate

Now that the action is out, a few minutes spent studying the grand piano's moving parts will be worthwhile.

Sustaining pedal

Depress the sustaining pedal and watch the dampers rise up immediately from the strings. Take your foot off and watch them fall back under their own weight. Follow the system through from beginning to end and the mechanism will become clear to you. Look inside the cavity where the action was housed and raise just one damper lever of the sustaining pedal system. Just one damper will rise off the strings. What your finger is doing is what the back end of the key does when it is in the piano.

Soft pedal

Look inside the piano, and at the rear centre of the keybed you will see a metal tongue sticking out. Depress the left-hand pedal and this tongue moves to one side, usually to the right. Go to the action, feel or look underneath the rear centre of the keyframe and you will discover a channel cut out of the wood. When the action is in position in the piano the tongue connects with this channel, so that when the pedal is depressed the keyboard moves to one side. The movement is just sufficient for the hammers to be sent a little off-line, causing those in the tri-chord region to strike only two strings, and those in the bi-chord area to strike only one string. The hammers in the bottom octave still manage to make contact with the single string. The result is a reduction in volume. Look inside the piano again. A strong spring screwed to one side of the inner case pushes the keyboard back to its normal position when the pedal is released.

The action

Depress a key with one hand and hold the palm of the other hand above the hammer at about string height, to stop it from over-riding. Note how the key capstan sets in motion the lever unit and how the jack throws the hammer—in many ways similar to the upright action. A little time spent investigating, and the basic principles of the grand's action will become clear.

Putting it all together again

You wouldn't put the action back in without cleaning away all the dust and foreign bodies. As cleaning is dealt with later in the text (pp. 17–19), we will assume here that everything is spick and span.

1. If the action felt tight and difficult on removal, then there may be some high spots on the keybed. Give-away signs would be shiny patches. Rub some household soap over these.

2. Place the action on the keybed. It needs to be positioned more to the right than to the left. (The keyblock at the bass end is about twice the width of that at the treble.)

3. Raise the front of the action a little and push carefully until the hammers are almost underneath and in line with the lid drop.

4. When about to 'go under the tunnel' with the action, remember not to touch any of the keys and to keep the front end raised a little.

5. With the fingers underneath the keybed, press home with the heels of the hands, just a little with the left and then the right, keeping the action as square to the piano as possible.

6. A final push with the thumbs, the fingers gripping under-neath, usually settles the action correctly.

7. Before re-fitting all the bits and pieces, the piano needs to be played to ensure that the action is properly seated, so try it out. Any Beethoven sonata will do.

Cleaning a grand piano

Now that you are familiar with the mechanism of the grand, and feel confident about removing its innards, a thorough cleaning service can be carried out.

The action, safely on a bench, will need to be separated from the keyframe so that the keys can be removed to expose the rails and the biggest deposits of dust. The action will have four standards, each with two screws. Unscrew them and lift off the action. All parts can then be cleaned as described on pp. 12–13.

That was easy, but putting the action back on can be tricky. When the action was removed, and its weight taken off the keys, the keys would have tipped down at the front, throwing the metal capstans a little off the perpendicular. Replacing the action whilst all the keys are in this position will result in a mis-alignment between the capstans and the whippen cushions (the undersides of the action units), and the keys will remain jammed down. To overcome this problem place a length of batten (the keyslip will be just right) along the back of the keys behind the back checks and ask an assistant to press the batten down, bringing the keys

Figure 1. Cleaning the grand soundboard

back up to normal. Now the action can be screwed back in. If you are working alone, try tying the batten down with a few pieces of string, and a little ingenuity.

Leaving the action where it is, clean the rest of the piano.

1.   Tie a length of thin wire to the corner of a dry duster. Place it on one side of the soundboard, feed the wire under the strings and pull the wire through to the other side.

2.   Using a narrow, blunt tool inserted between the strings, find a well-padded part of the duster and guide around the soundboard, using your other hand to pull the wire. (*see* Figure 1).

3.   Work the debris forward so that it falls into the box where the action is normally kept.

4.   When all the dust has been cleaned away with a brush and vacuum, repeat the operation, but this time with a slightly damp cloth soaked in a weak solution of vinegar and water.

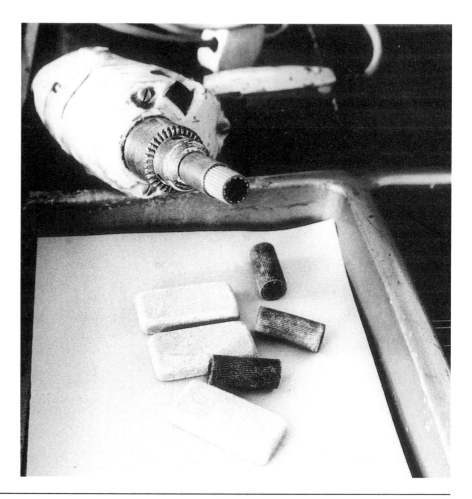

Figure 2. Using burnishing rubbers

Because of its large, flat top a grand piano is often used as a dumping ground for anything that won't conveniently fit elsewhere, flower pots in particular, and what a handy place it is to leave a drink when the telephone rings. But there is a price to pay for this; rusted strings and tuning pins present quite an eyesore when the lid is fully opened. Similar sights are found in uprights of course, but as the panels are usually kept in position they are not on public view.

The pins and strings can be brightened with burnishing rubbers. An electric drill attachment will take the cylindrical rubbers for the pins, and flat, hand-held rubbers are used on the strings (but not on the copper windings). Place sheets of newspaper on the soundboard (today's edition facing the right way as it is a long job) and remove the action. (*See* Figure 2.)

Action repairs

THE UPRIGHT ACTION

Before attempting a repair to the upright action it is advisable that you should understand both its mechanical arrangement and its type. There are several types of action but, whatever the design may be, the basic principles remain the same. Study the following list and decide to which type yours belongs.

Type A: overstrung, underdamped, tape action.

In this design the hammers will be offset to correspond to the lines of the strings. The dampers cannot be seen easily, but by looking over the top of the action you will see them just below the hammers. The tapes, made of white fabric, will have reinforcements on the ends nearest you, often coloured red, and will be fitted over wires.

Type B: overstrung, overdamped, tape action.

The offset hammer arrangement and the tapes will be the same as in Type A, but the dampers are easy to see, being set above the hammers, and having long wires running down in front of the action.

Type C: vertical strung, underdamped, tape action.

The hammers will not be offset, but square, and will look evenly spaced. Damping and taping will be as in Type A.

Type D: vertical strung, overdamped, tape action.

Stringing and tape arrangements as in Type C, but damping system as in Type B.

Type E: loop and wire action.

This arrangement is usually found in vertically strung, overdamped pianos of days gone by. It preceded the more modern tape design, and a peep into the innards of the action will show a length of wire hooked on to a loop made of cord.

Type F: sticker action.

Stickers are employed on tall pianos and can be used with any type of action. They are simply extension pieces between the keys and action and on observation their function will be quite obvious.

Your action will have a similar design to one of those above, but variations and permutations do occur. Figure 3 shows the parts of a typical upright piano action.

Select a key which when played seems in perfect order. Depress the key, which is balanced in the middle as in a 'see-saw', and you will see that as the front end goes down, the far end goes up. Watch how the capstan at the far end of the key makes contact with the lever, either directly or via a sticker, which in turn causes the jack to rise. The jack makes contact with the underside of the hammer butt, throwing the hammer towards the strings. The jack does not keep in contact with the butt, but is stopped by the let-off button (let-off buttons are fixed to a rail fitted on the action frame). The lever section now settles back down to rest whilst the hammer continues the journey under its

Figure 3. Upright action parts
Hammer section
A hammer
B hammer shank
C hammer butt
D hammer-butt flange
E back stop shank
F back stop
G bridle tape
Lever section
H lever
I lever flange
J back check
K back-check wire
L bridle wire
M jack
N jack flange
O jack knuckle
P jack spring
Q damper spoon
Damper section
R damper lever
S damper head
T damper wire (underdamped action)
U damper flange
V damper spring

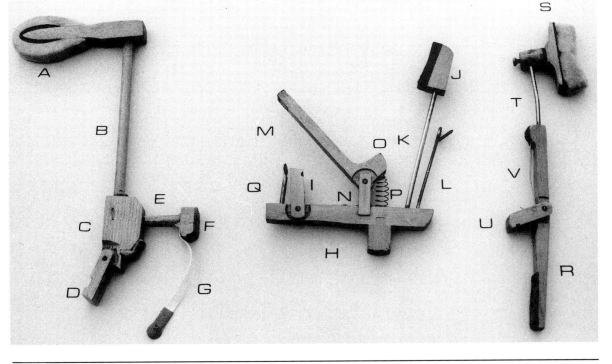

own impetus. The hammer, on returning, but before it finally comes to rest, is 'checked', or steadied, by the back check.

By looking over the top of the action, and playing a key at the same time, it will soon become apparent how a damper is brought away from the strings when the key is depressed, and returns to damp the strings when the key rises back up to its normal position. Depress the right-hand pedal and notice the upright rod of the pedal system rising to lift the damper rail, thereby causing all the dampers to leave the strings. Take your foot off the pedal and the dampers return to the strings.

Remove the action from the piano, secure it firmly on a table and make sure that there is access to both back and front. **Note**: the methods of repairing to be described may not be in strict accordance with those used by the trade. For instance, a professional working on a quality piano may well boil his own glue and apply it with a camel-hair brush. The methods here suggest using a tube of ordinary transparent household glue for wood to wood, and white adhesive for felt to wood, both being expedient and adequate.

Removing a defective action part for repair.

To remove an action part belonging to either Type A or C, first unhook the tape at the front. Standing behind the action, unscrew the flange which holds the lever section in place. The lever, now being free from the tape and the rail, should be held in one hand to stop it from falling. Place it to one side on the table, being careful not to lose the jack spring. Standing at the front end of the action push the hammer forward and the butt flange will be seen. Unscrew and place the hammer section on the table.

Types B and D are generally much easier to remove. First unhook the tape at the front and spring the front damper wire from out of the lever. It is important that you bend the damper wire out of the lever; do not depress the lever, as it may snap. The screws securing both the hammer and lever sections are at the rear, and it doesn't matter which you unscrew first.

Several variations occur with loop and wire style actions as in Type E. If both the hammer and lever sections are still joined together by the loop and wire they may have to be taken out as one, for it can be difficult to separate them whilst still in position in the action. In order to do this the button rail may have to be removed. Once out, the two sections can be separated for repair.

Fitting a new hammer shank

The accepted method of fitting a new hammer shank is to steam out the broken ends of the shank from the butt and the hammer and to replace with a new shank of equal diameter. Danger lurks here, for damage can be caused by softening the wood and the

Figure 4. Sawing off the broken shank

Figure 5. Drilling to receive the new shank

hammer felt. An alternative method of sawing and drilling can be used.

Using a hacksaw blade, saw off the broken ends of the shank flush with the butt and hammer and finish neatly with a file or sandpaper (*see* Figure 4).

Mark both the butt and the hammer with a pencil to show the exact centres where the holes are to be drilled. Using a pilot drill of about 1.5mm ($\frac{1}{16}$in.), and fitted with a handle, bore holes in each part to a depth of 6mm ($\frac{1}{4}$in.). With an intermediate size drill of about 3mm ($\frac{1}{8}$in.), widen the holes but do not make them any deeper. Finally, using a 5mm ($\frac{3}{16}$in.) drill, complete the boring operation on both parts (*see* Figure 5).

A new shank of 5mm ($\frac{3}{16}$in.) will be needed. This may be of a smaller diameter than the original, but it allows for a greater margin of error should your drilling be slightly off-centre. Roll

Figure 6. Marking for depth

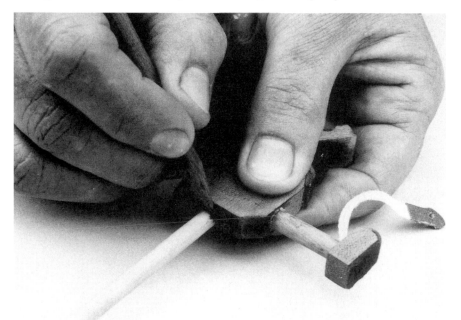

the shank on a flat surface to check that it is round and straight, reject it if it appears to be bumpy, as a twisted shank will cause all sorts of problems. Fit the shank into the butt and mark with a pencil (*see* Figure 6), so that a check can be made later to see that it is fully inserted. Take the shank out and lightly roll the end, as far as the pencil mark, on a flat file or piece of sandpaper to give it a key for glueing, making sure that no wood is removed nor the diameter of the shank reduced. Fit into the butt, checking the pencil mark to ensure that is fully home. Now place the butt and shank in position in the action, taking care that the flange is correctly located. Screw the flange into position if you're not sure that it's aligned properly. Mark with a pencil where the shank needs to be cut off, erring on the long side, because if it's too long it can easily be filed down to size.

Figure 7. Measuring for correct length of shank

Remove the shank and butt from the action and saw off at the pencil mark. Now fit the hammer onto the shank, marking the shank again with a pencil to check that it is fully inserted. Fit the complete unit to the action and square off. When satisfied that the shank length and general alignment is correct, remove the unit from the action and separate the parts. Give a key for glueing as far as the pencil mark.

Squeeze a drop of glue into each drilled-out hole and fit everything together, making sure that the same ends of the shank are used as when dry-fitted, and that they are tapped fully home

Figure 8. Squaring off

to the pencil marks. Act quickly if a quick-drying glue is being used so that any squaring-up can be done before the glue has dried. Place in the action and screw up, squaring off if necessary with a pair of long-nose pliers.

Off-set hammers

Steaming out the broken shank from both parts and replacing it with a new shank of equal diameter will eliminate the tricky problem of boring at an angle. Those with woodworking skills and elaborate electrical equipment for off-set boring should machine drill using the pilot only, the rest of the operation should be completed by hand.

Fitting new bridle tapes

Figure 9. Fitting a new bridle tape

New tapes will always be longer than needed and should be cut to size using a neighbouring tape which is still intact as a guide. Ream the hole in the tape end a little and glue to the butt as shown in Figure 9. If the new tape end is too thick to fit on to the wire then prise open the wire a little with a screwdriver.

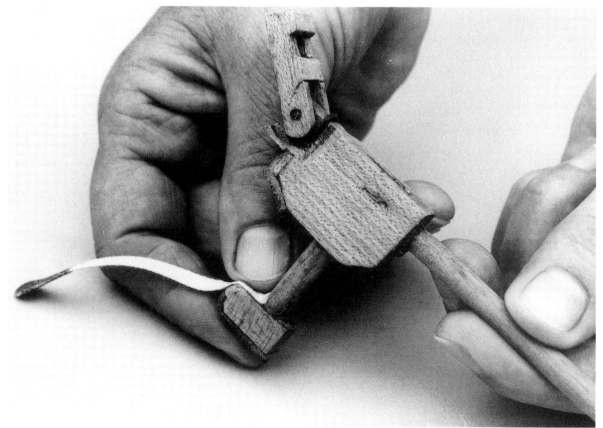

Re-fixing loose hammer felt

This problem occurs usually on the underside of the hammer. Glue and tack back together with two panel pins, bending the pins over before finally driving them home.

Figure 10. Re-fixing loose hammer-felt

Replacing missing notch felt

Remove the hammer section and clean and sand the surface. Cut and glue a piece of felt of suitable thickness; too thick a pad will cause jack problems after re-fitting.

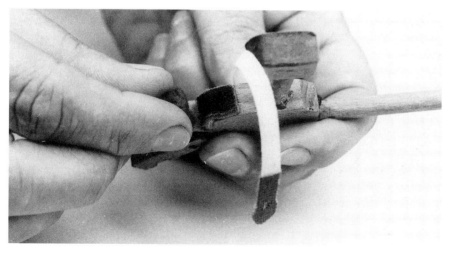

Figure 11. Fitting new felt to notch

Flanges

The most common problem with a flange is a loose centre pin having come part of the way out, and should this occur with the butt flange, then the hammer will wobble all over the place. (If the symptom is hammer wobble then check first that the flange is screwed in tightly.) Remove the part, take the pin out and score the pin with a hacksaw blade or light file as this may give it sufficient bite to hold tight. If scoring is not successful then a pin the next size up will be needed. When fitting the parts back together make sure that they are properly lined up or something will surely break. If a small woodworker's vice is used the parts must be held very gently indeed.

A broken flange cannot be repaired and, if this is the problem, a replacement of the same pattern will have to be obtained. If the piano does not warrant too much attention then an exchange of parts may be made taking a flange from one of the ends, remembering that if it is the butt flange that is broken then the hammers will need exchanging also. This practice, known as 'robbing the ends', is frowned upon by the trade. However, it is your piano and you are not getting paid.

A tight flange, resulting in slow movements of the section, may be eased by applying a touch of piano-action lubricant with an artist's brush. Pour a small amount of lubricant, sufficient for immediate use, into a small container such as an egg cup. Apply the lubricant, leave overnight, then gently work the part with the fingers. Do not pour back any left-over lubricant into the bottle.

Figure 12. Applying a touch of lubricant

Jack springs

The most common problems occuring with jack springs are that they may be weak, broken or missing. Ideally, you should remove the lever section and fit a new spring of the same size (there are a few different sizes). If the piano is at death's door and a replacement spring is not available then stealing a good one from the end is hardly a crime.

Loop and wire

The loop and wire in the action of that name perform the same functions as the tape and jack spring in the tape action. The system has not been used in pianos since the early 1900s and broken loops and wires are now very common.

Loop cord can be purchased should any loops be broken, but in an emergency strong twine can be used. Remove the part and dislodge the little plug from the hole in which the cord was fitted. Clean away the dried glue using a suitable small tool such as a piece of wire. Cut a length of cord a little longer than needed and pull through using a piece of very thin wire bent in half.

Using a narrow dowel with an outside diameter the same as the inside diameter of the loop (a good guess can be made by looking at the loop next door), pull the cord tight around the dowel and insert a splinter of wood (such as the end of a matchstick) into the hole, having first dipped it in glue. Remove the dowel. When dry, cut off the excess with a razor blade. If this seems a bit tricky then just tie a knot in the cord sufficiently large enough to stop it from being pulled through. The important point is that the loop is near enough the correct size.

A broken loop wire cannot be repaired but must be replaced with one of the same length, as there are different sizes. Take out the action part, remove the broken wire—noting how it was fitted—and fit the new wire in the same way. The fitting end of the new wire may be a little longer than is needed and will have to be cut to size. The whole operation is tricky but it can be done, using patience, a steady hand and a pair of long-nose pliers. If all this seems frightening then leaving the parts in the action and experimenting with a packet of assorted elastic bands may bring success.

If the piano is in such a state that a priest could do more for it than a tuner, then rob a part in good order from either the top or bottom, explaining to the family that the swap was justified 'as we hardly ever play the notes on the ends anyway'.

Figure 13. Types of dampers

Figure 13. Types of dampers

Problems with dampers

The three most common types of dampers are shown in Figure 13. The 'clip' **(1)** clips over a single bass string. The 'wedge' **(2)** wedges between the two bass strings as in the bi-chord section and the 'flat' type **(3)** damps the remaining tri-chord section. This is the design of the underdamper system. Flat dampers are often used throughout the range in most pianos with overdamped actions. The reason for the different shapes is obvious from the above and only a damper of the correct shape should be fitted if one is missing. A missing damper felt can usually be found in the bottom of the piano, unless the mice have got there first. To re-fit, unlock the action then, do not remove it, but bring it forward a little so as to have room to work. Sand and glue both surfaces, fit the two parts together and push the action home, lining up the damper felt with the strings, which will act as a clamp. Ordinary transparent tube glue is too messy for this job, it is better to use a white glue.

New parts can be purchased to replace broken damper parts but if the piano has seen better days then why not exchange the complete damper unit with the last at the treble end? If you feel guilty about such malpractice then do it quickly, when nobody is looking.

Re-fitting to the action

Refer to these instructions after completing your repairs. The instructions assume that you are right-handed. Reverse if left-handed.

Types A and C

From the front, place the hammer section in position and balance the flange screw on the end of a screwdriver as shown in Figure 14. Screw in the hammer section. Do not overtighten any flange screw as the part will shatter. It is quite sufficient to turn the screwdriver with your fingers until the screw feels firm.

Figure 14. Refitting the hammer section, type A

When re-fitting the lever section it may be necessary to bend the damper spoon out of the way a little, remembering to return it to its original setting after completion. Standing at the back of the action, place the lever section in position, using those parts on either side as a guide for lining up. Hold the flange in position with your left-hand thumb, and with your left-hand fingers activate the lever so as to throw the hammer forward. This will cause the damper spoon to move away from the flange and thus provide a little more room to work in. Using your right-hand fingers, place the screw in position and tighten with the screwdriver.

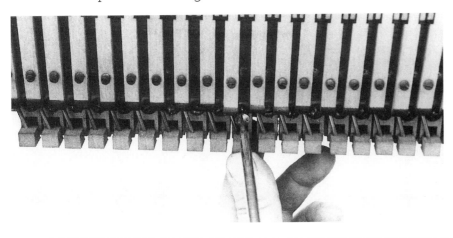

Figure 15. Re-fitting the lever section, type A

When re-fitting the bridle tape to the wire, use a screwdriver (or similar tool) in your right hand to depress the jack knuckle so that the jack is not jammed under the butt. Keep the section in position by letting it rest on your right-hand fingers carefully and fit the tape with your left hand.

Figure 16. Re-fitting the tape

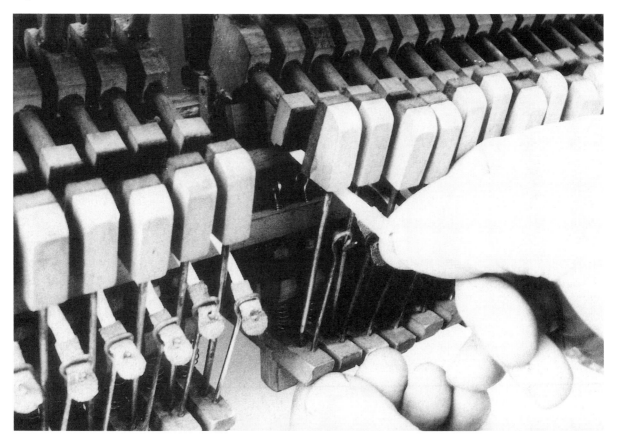

Types B and D

Either section can be secured first and the tape re-fitted in the same manner as for Types A and C. When locating the front damper wire to the lever, remember not to press the lever down but hold it firm and spring the wire in.

Type E

The hammer and lever sections of a loop and wire style action are best re-fitted to the action by joining them together first and putting them in as one, though this may necessitate the removal of the button rail. Extremely good eyesight and a very steady hand are needed if they are to be joined together after being installed.

A GENERAL OVERHAUL

If several notch felts and tapes are missing then it will be only a matter of time before the rest will decay and fall off. In circumstances such as this it is wise to renew the lot in one go. If one part of the action has already been removed, successfully repaired and replaced then performing a general overhaul is not a terrifying prospect—just the same activity performed 85 times. If the amount of time involved causes concern then, as a guide, removing four sections, fitting new notch felts and tapes and re-fitting all to the action would take about an hour. Of course, if the problem is of a more complicated nature, such as broken loop cords, then it takes longer. An overhaul can be a tedious and time-consuming operation but to see and feel the action under the fingers after it has a face-lift, not to mention the hundreds of pounds saved, is very rewarding.

Figure 17. Ensuring correct re-alignment

Overhaul procedure

With the action firmly secured on a table and, counting from the bottom, remove the four hammer and lever sections as shown in Figure 17. Place the parts, in order, on the table and number them, with a pencil, 5, 6, 7 and 8 (Nos 1–4 stay in the piano). Clean the parts (an old toothbrush is handy), wipe with a damp cloth and dry. Using a small brush, clean between the rails of the action that area where the parts have just been removed. When carrying out repairs it is expedient to complete one type of operation at a time, e.g., cut and fit four new pads, cut and fit four new tapes. After carrying out the necessary repairs replace section No. 5 and line up the hammer and lever sections with part No. 4. Now re-fit section No. 8 and line up with No. 9. Finally re-fit the two remaining sections. Following this procedure will ensure that hammer and lever alignment and tape lengths are correct.

Remove the parts numbered 1, 2, 3 and 4, complete the repairs and when re-fitting start with No. 4, aligning with No. 5, then re-fit Nos 3, 2 and 1. To maintain correct alignment, you should remove next Nos 13, 14, 15 and 16, do the necessary repairs and re-fit starting with No. 13. The pattern is now obvious and common sense will dictate what to do should a break in the stringing occur, as is the case in overstrung pianos. The procedure can be reversed and a start made at the top end if you prefer: the top end is free of dampers and you will gain confidence before eventually arriving at the damper system.

Figure 18. Hammers kept firmly in place

Should the action be well and truly moth-eaten then it is possible that after being placed on the table many of the lever sections will hang down because of missing or broken tapes. Do not despair. Find a small group where the tapes are still intact, leave them in position, and remove for repair a few at a time from either side of that group, always re-fitting first the repaired parts that are next to those still left in the action. To maintain a guide for alignment, it may be necessary to 'patch' by replacing, a little here, a little there, etc.

When working on an overdamped action, remove the damper system by unscrewing the top rail, being careful not to lose any of the front wire washers, and rest it on blocks on a table, so as not to damage the damper heads. If the hammer-rest rail felt is in a sorry state, and it probably will be, now is the time to renew it. Before removing the hammer-rest rail, tie a length of string from one standard to the other to keep the hammers in place (Figure 18). The new felt should be then glued on using a white glue.

White keys

To re-fit a white key top which has come adrift, or to fit a new covering, first remove the key and sand the surfaces to be glued, making sure that all the old glue is removed. (A new top will not need sanding.) To maintain an even, flat surface the key should be sanded on a block and the movements of the hand kept as straight as possible. Apply a thin, even coat of glue to both surfaces (too thick an application on an uneven, pitted surface will show up as ripples on the white key top), allow to become tacky

Figure 19. Preparing a key on a sanding block

and clamp together. The clamps which hold in place the net of a table-tennis set are useful for this. If no clamps are available then hold together in your fingers for a few minutes.

Figure 20. Marking a white key top for cutting

White key tops of the plastic kind can be cut from a sheet of key covering material, using a sheet large enough to provide many tops. Cut a length just a little too big, allow for the overhang at the front, and place, sunny-side up, in position on the key. Pencil on the outline of the key beneath. Cut at the pencil marks using strong scissors and dry fit to the key. When you are satisfied that a reasonably good fit has been achieved, glue together and allow to dry hard. When dry, trim the edges with a light file or sandpaper, round off the corners of the overhang and remove any excess glue (*see* Figure 21).

Key fronts can be purchased in convenient strips, each long enough to do several fronts. Cut off to size, clean the front of the key, glue on the new key front and when dry trim with a file or sandpaper.

Ivory key tops are always in two halves, 'heads' and 'tails'. Do not fit a brilliant white plastic head or tail to a yellowing ivory keyboard, for it will stand out just as much as when the part was missing. Second-hand ivory heads and tails and look-alike imitation ivory sets can be purchased and are not expensive.

If the keyboard is a real eyesore, with some whites missing, some broken and some so badly chipped at the front that a visit to the dentist wouldn't do any harm, then a complete keyboard recovering operation would be worth considering. White tops in moulded sets, ready cut to shape, with or without fronts, can be purchased quite cheaply.

White plastic key coverings can be removed by applying heat, or burning off, with a wet cloth at the ready to put out the flame. To remove an ivory top, cover with a wet cloth then, using a hot iron, press on the cloth to soften the glue. Unless the covering is very loose do not attempt to prise it off with a knife lest you damage the wooden surface of the key.

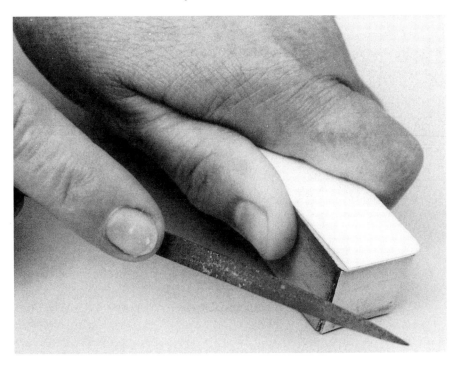

Figure 21. Giving the key top a final trim

Black keys (sharps)

Black key tops do not present as many problems as do white key tops. They have no coverings and do not break. A sharp which has come away can easily be glued back on: simply sand both surfaces, glue together and clean away any excess when dry.

The problem of a missing sharp somewhere in the central playing area of the piano can be overcome by using one of the following methods.

1. Break off the bottom sharp on the piano, prepare the surfaces and glue to the key with the missing top.

2. Use a sharp from a scrap piano and fit to the bottom key. If it is too long then it can be cut to size and if too short, or of a different design, then by fitting it at the bottom end of the piano its appearance will not be so noticeable.

3. A new sharp can be made to order. This means breaking off the bottom sharp to send away as a pattern. If the missing sharp is in the middle region of the keyboard and the piano is needed for daily practice then remove yet another sharp from the bottom and re-fit in the middle.

4. A new part can readily be made from a piece of scrap hardwood. Cut to size and shape, stain black and finish with black gloss (not the underside of course). Allow to dry, and fit.

A broken key

This is a problem. When a key breaks it always does so at the point where it fits over the balance rail pin, and there is very little material to work with. Do not sand the jagged edges but leave intact so that they can be interlocked. Place the two halves on a flat surface and, using an instant contact glue (following the instructions given), fit the pieces together and hold firm with your fingers for about a minute. Using a fairly wide roll of adhesive tape (such as Sellotape), wrap diagonally around the damaged area, just overlapping as you go. Avoid crinkling the tape at the sides and cut off at either the top or bottom side of the key. Leave to dry for a while then cut away the tape from around the hole with a razor blade and clean up inside.

All kinds of inventive pinning and clipping can be tried but are usually unsuccessful and each such attempt further weakens the key. A channel can be cut out of each side of the key, bridging the broken area, then a strip of veneer of perfect fit can be glued and slotted into each channel and sanded flush when dry, though such a repair could not be expected from someone unskilled in craftwork.

But all is not lost. A new key can be made from a pattern.

Wooden capstan

The wooden capstan is the most common in use and a breakage often occurs in very old pianos. If the broken capstan is somewhere in the middle region of the piano then first exchange with one from either the top or bottom. (These continued suggestions of swapping are not criminal but practical as they allow the piano to be played in its most usual regions, the problem being relegated to the extremities where the repair can be considered at leisure.) Using another capstan as a guide, cut a new one to size from a piece of dowel of the same diameter, drill for fitting to the wire, drill the regulating holes, and cut and fit a new felt cap (if appropriate to the design). While the action is removed it is worth checking all the felt tops and replacing or re-glueing as necessary and, as capstans of this type are often rusted in, ease them all by turning and coaxing with the fingers.

Figure 22. The pedal system

The pedals

With the panels removed, study the pedal system for a few moments and the mechanical arrangements will soon become clear.

The right-hand, or 'loud' pedal system, as it is usually (though incorrectly) called, is similar in all pianos whatever the damper design. When the pedal is depressed the horizontal rod connects with the vertical rod which raises the damper rail, allowing all the dampers to come away free from the strings. Playing with the dampers free from the strings sustains the sound, hence the correct name for the pedal, the 'sustaining' pedal.

The left-hand, or 'soft', pedal system, can be one of two designs.

1. On all pianos with an underdamped action, and sometimes on those with an overdamped action, depress the pedal and the vertical rod moves the hammer-rest rail closer to the strings. The hammers, having less distance to travel, provide a quieter sound.

2. The usual system to be found in most pianos with an overdamped action employs a celeste rail, brought into use by two horizontal and two vertical rods. Depressing the pedal brings the two vertical rods into play, raising the celeste rail, to which is glued a strip of soft felt. The felt comes between the hammers and the strings, muting the sound.

Adjusting nut

The vertical rods should be just underneath and ready for lifting either the damper rail (right-hand pedal) or in the case of the soft pedal (underdamped action), the hammer-rest rail. This situation is determined by the adjusting nut, where the most usual problem is rust, which can make the nut impossible to move with the fingers. Wire brush away the rust and apply releasing oil, using a cloth to catch any spillage, and to wipe away oil where it is not wanted. After the oil has had time to penetrate, work the nut loose with a pair of pliers.

Pedal bolt

If the bolt which takes the adjusting nut is broken, purchase a long bolt of suitable diameter, together with a nut. The pedal hinge will have to be unscrewed so that the head of the bolt can be fitted underneath, and a metal washer may be necessary. Measure the length of bolt required, saw off the new bolt to length, round off the sawn-off edge with a file, put into place, fit a felt washer and finally add the nut. If the hinge is underneath the bottom board then the piano will have to be put on its back to do the repair. See the section on casework renovation (p. 123) for how to lay a piano down.

Pedal hinge

A loose fitting in the pedal hinge will show up when the pedal wobbles from side to side, or may even jam underneath the rebate (that part at the bottom of the piano which has been cut away to receive the pedal). If the system is of the nut and bolt type (not to be confused with the adjusting nut), then the problem is usually easily solved. Either the nut has come loose or the bolt has broken. Tighten or renew as the case may be.

If the design consists of cone-shaped fittings and sockets then the cones, if well worn, will become loose and may slip out. Removing the hinge and squeezing together in a vice may solve the problem, but will create a greater problem should something snap. Should the wear be excessive then it is possible to drill through the whole system, on a workbench of course, and re-fit with a nut and bolt.

The soft pedal is rarely used and will proably be in sound working order. Why not do a swap with parts from the soft pedal and worry about the matter tomorrow?

Broken 'U' spring

This spring provides resistance when the pedal is depressed, and causes it to return to the resting position when the foot is removed.

A new spring is inexpensive and fitting is straightforward. A more immediate repair is use a stout coil spring and fit this between the bottom board and the horizontal rod. If the coil spring is not long enough, then mount it on a small wooden block and secure by screwing it to the bottom board. A hollow, cut out of the block, will keep the spring in position.

Figure 23. A makeshift spring

Vertical rod

The vertical rod becoming disconnected from the horizontal rod is quite a common ocurrence. Gluing both sides of a felt pad and then fitting it between the two sections would certainly look like a neat repair but, unless a superb bond is achieved, this will not last for very long. A more effective method is to glue a piece of felt to the sides of both rods and reinforce with drawing pins, as shown in Figure 24.

A missing or snapped vertical rod is an easy problem to deal with. Vertical rods, whether round or square, are usually tapered throughout their entire lengths. Purchase a length of dowel of suitable diameter; there is no need to taper the whole length, but shape just enough at the top end so that it will fit into the guide block.

Figure 24. Re-connecting the rods

Celeste rails

Celeste rails are usually secured into slots cut in the vertical rods, and have a nasty habit of jumping out, particularly when the piano is moved. A couple of cardboard wedges should cure this.

Worn felt should be replaced only by celeste rail felt, as anything thicker or harder may eliminate the sound altogether. Glue with a white adhesive, gently pulling as you go to avoid bunching the felt. Leave about 25mm (1in.), showing above the rail.

A missing celeste rail can be replaced easily using a piece of batten 35mm (1⅜in.) wide and 6mm (¼in.) thick. Cut to length.

THE GRAND ACTION

The methods of repairing and renewing action parts such as hammer shanks, felts, key coverings etc., have already been fully explained above.

A frustrating problem can occur in a grand action when you wish to remove a complete action unit for repair. The action is held in the action frame by one flange screw, to be found at the rear of the hammer-rest rail. Once the screw is out the unit is free of fixing but it may not be able to pass through the two action rails. Pull to the rear and the jack heel can't pass the let-off dowel because the flange end is halted by the hammer-rest rail. Manoeuvre to the front and the flange can't gain exit from the

Figure 25. The grand piano action unit
A hammer flange
B drop screw
C roller
D lever flange
E jack regulating screw
F repetition lever regulating screw
G repetition lever spring regulating screw
H whippen cushion

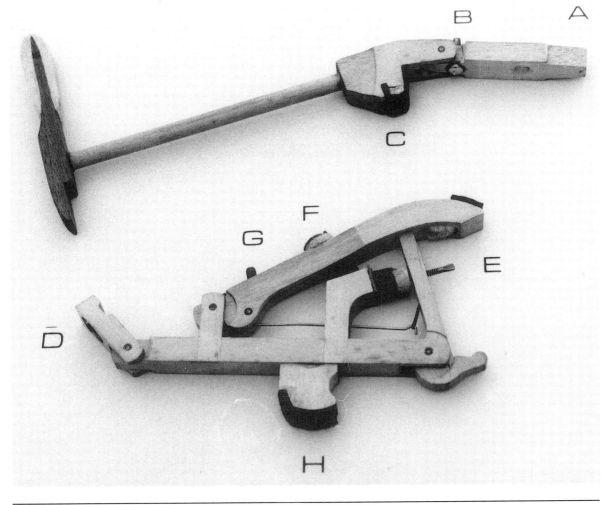

hammer-rest rail because the whippen cushion can't ride over the key capstan. Totally trapped!

Turn down the metal capstan to increase clearance. This usually works, but if there is still no escape you will need to remove the main action rail (i.e. the rail that the hammer flanges are screwed to). If the sight of 88 hammers dangling by their flanges worries you then have someone support them with the keyslip.

Watch out for small, paper shims falling out when you unscrew the lever and hammer flanges, and try to put them back in the same position when re-fitting. They will have been put in purposely by a previous technician to square the parts up properly.

The piano doctor

Diagnosing the reason for a problem in an everyday household situation such as the family car refusing to start or the cat's sudden loss of appetite is usually more difficult than effecting the cure. Pinpointing a piano's ills is surprisingly easy, provided that you follow through a systematic process of elimination. **Note**: in the following procedures, only those repairs *not* catered for in the preceding section will be explained.

The cause of an ailment should be isolated quickly to either the action or the key. Activate the action by flicking the lever from underneath with the finger as shown in Figure 26. If the system works satisfactorily then the fault is in the key. If the problem remains then the fault is in the action.

Figure 26. Isolating the problem

UPRIGHT PIANOS

Ailment

Hammer not rising or very lttle movement

Causes	*Remedies*
1. Foreign object under key	Remove
2. Key: broken at the balance rail. (The front end goes down. The far end remains still)	Repair
3. Capstan: missing, damaged, out of line or not adjusted high enough	Service as necessary
4. Capstan: felt top missing	Fit new top
5. Jack spring: missing, broken, weak or dislodged. Alternatively, if you are dealing with a loop and wire action, either the loop or the wire could be broken. If the trouble lies somewhere here, the jack will not be in position underneath the butt but will be forward, i.e. towards you, rather than in line with the others	Repair or replace as the case may be
6. Jack flange: tight. A faint scuffing noise will be heard. The jack, not properly settled underneath, will be unable to deliver a good 'uppercut' to the butt and will glance off	Using an artist's brush, apply a touch of action lubricant to the flange, leaving the action in position, and work the part vigorously with the fingers a few times
7. Jack flange: either broken or with a dislodged centre pin. Either fault can cause the jack to rise at an angle and miss the butt	Refer to 'Action repairs' (p. 28)
8. Lever flange: tight	Try lubricant
9. Back check: too close to the back stop. This halts the rise of the lever section	Bend the back check wire back a little
10. Hammer: rubbing tight on to an adjacent hammer, particularly in the off-set region of an overstrung piano	Re-align
11. Foreign object on the rail between the hammers and the dampers in an underdamped action	Remove

12. Tape: too tight — Push in the bridle wire a little

13. Butt flange: tight — Lubricate

14. Butt flange: broken, or centre pin partly out — Service as appropriate

15. Notch felt: missing. This will cause the jack to jam under the butt — Cut and glue new felt

Ailment

No repetition. A key will play only once, or just a few times.

Causes	*Remedies*
1. Key: not rising fully back up	Ease the key by gently squeezing the bushing as shown in Figure 27. The trade uses a special tool with parallel jaws for this activity but a satisfactory result can be obtained with a pair of long-nose pliers
2. Jack spring: weak	Renew
3. Jack flange: tight	Lubricate
4. Lever flange: tight	Lubricate
5. Butt flange: tight	Lubricate

N.B. A weak jack spring or tight flange will not allow the jack to re-settle very quickly

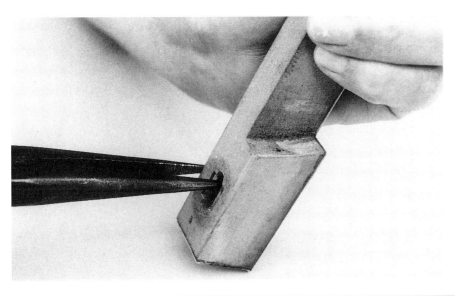

Figure 27. Easing the key bushing

Ailment

Hammer not returning after striking string

Causes	*Remedies*
1. Front end of key not rising back up	Ease
2. Tape: broken	'Clip on' tapes are handy and can be fitted without having to remove the action. Adjust the length by twisting around the brass clip, and ream out the hole a little. If the hammer is blocked on the strings, in order to fit the tape depress the jack knuckle as shown in Figure 28
3. Damper (overdamped action): the hammer may have jammed underneath the damper, at a point where it has nearly reached the strings	Unlock the action and pull it forward far enough to get your hand in so that you can raise the damper a little with the fingers
4. Hammer: touching an adjacent hammer	Re-align
5. Butt flange: tight	Lubricate
6. Strings missing, causing the hammer to jam	Strings are dealt with in Chapter 5

Figure 28. 'Clip-on' tapes

Ailment

Hammer slow to return

Causes	*Remedies*
1. Key: returns slowly to normal position because of tight bushing	Ease with pliers
2. Butt flange: tight	Lubricate
3. Lever flange: tight	Lubricate

Ailment

Sticking keys

Causes	*Remedies*
1. Pins: rusted	Clean
2. Front rail pin: these are oval shaped and are sometimes called 'cricket bats'. If set at too sharp an angle then the keys may stick	Adjust as illustrated in Figure 29

Figure 29. Adjusting the front-rail pin

3. Key bushing: tight. This may also be the cause of a sluggish return to the normal position	Ease with pliers

4.	Key: touching an adjacent key: either one or both keys may be at fault	Remove and sand surfaces
5.	Key front: loose and fouling on keyslip	Re-glue
6.	Corroded lead weights on the key, or an adjacent key	Remove key and sand
7.	Key dip: if there is too much dip then the key will jam on the front rail pin	Correct with paper washers. This is explained under the section on regulating (pp. 104–5)

Ailment

A key refuses to go down or only goes down with great difficulty

Causes		*Remedies*
1.	A foreign object has found its way in— a coin if it's your lucky day	Take out the key and remove object
2.	Action: jammed. If the lever section cannot move then the capstan cannot move and the key cannot move	Investigate thoroughly. The chances are that the problem is caused by a missing notch felt. Replace as described on p. 27

Ailment

Key remains down and returns only when an adjacent key is played; two adjacent keys go down together

Causes		*Remedies*
1.	The keys are touching because the wood has warped on one or both keys	Remove and sand
2.	Lead weight slugs: corroded and swollen	Remove keys and sand
3.	Sticky substance between the keys	Clean
4.	Small object between the keys, e.g. a needle	Remove

Some mysterious happenings

Ailment

A number of adjacent white keys stick

Causes	*Remedies*
1. The fact that only white keys are affected provides the clue. They all extend as far as the keyslip whereas the black keys do not. Ease the keyslip forward with your fingers and the keys will pop back up to their normal position. Either the keyslip has warped inwards or paint, or varnish, has found its way in	Remove the affected keys, and one or two more from either side, and sand the inside of the keyslip. If the problem still persists after sanding then you may need to insert small wedges between the keyslip and the keybed to counteract the inward spring of the keyslip

Ailment

Depress key and the wrong note sounds

Causes	*Remedies*
The capstan may be be bent, activating the lever next door, or, the jack flange pin may have come part of the way out, causing the jack to hit the butt next door	Straighten the capstan or re-fit the jack pin

Ailment

Depress key and two hammers rise

Causes	*Remedies*
As above	As above

Ailment

Play a black key and an adjacent white key goes down with it

Causes	*Remedies*
The back end white of the white key covering is proud of the key, and touching the front end of the black key	Trim the white key covering at the back of the head

Ailment

Play a black key and the white keys on either side go down with it

Causes	*Remedies*
Either the white key coverings need trimming at the back of the heads, or, more probably, the black key top is too far forward	Sand the front end so that it doesn't foul any more

Ailment

A generally sluggish action and keyboard

Causes and Remedies

This annoying condition can be found on all types of pianos, old and not so old. A damp environment is nearly always the cause, and lack of use will add to the problem. The symptoms are found in the action and keys at the treble end, outside of the damper influence. A slow, sluggish response is experienced each time the piano is played in this region and so many keys and action parts become stuck fast that further playing is impossible. However, the region within the damper field may be reasonably free when the sustaining pedal is not used but becomes as lethargic as the treble end when the pedal is used. The reason for this is that a key, or action part, in the damper region, has the advantage of extra weight afforded by either the damper spring (in an underdamped action) or the front wire assembly (in an overdamped action). This weight is suffient to tip the balance when the pedal is 'off', but depress the pedal and the damper rail is lifted, removing the extra weight.

If your piano reacts in the manner described then it is suffering from tight key bushings and/or tight action flanges. Having to ease all the keys is not too formidable a task—just a couple of hours' work. Removing action parts and easing just a few flanges is worthwhile if it cures the problem, but easing all the flanges is a massive undertaking. There are three flanges per action unit. Multiplying this by the number of units, 85, will amount to 255 operations. Sticker actions may well have 5 flanges per unit. Multiply this by 85 and you will be faced with 425 flanges to be eased, one at a time.

Before setting out on such a marathon I would advise that just two or three keys and action units be eased, replaced and tried. If successful then continue. If there is no improvement, then what a waste of time to continue! The flanges will need re-bushing and re-pinning, a delicate and highly skilled repair which can only be carried out at a professional workshop. This is a major overhaul, very expensive, and only warranted on a good quality piano.

If you are really desperate and crying out for help, then stand the action in the airing cupboard for a week and lay the keys on the windowsill next to the tomatoes.

Ailment

All the black keys jam

Causes	*Remedies*
This usually happens after the piano has been moved, or, after the top front panel and fallboard have been removed and on replacing the fallboard has not been seated properly	Re-seat the fallboard

Ailment

Unwanted noises in the keys and action

Isolating the problem

Not many owners of older pianos have the pleasure of hearing only the beautiful sounds of vibrating strings when they sit down to play. Irritating noises are usually in attendance, and most, if not all of these noises can be dealt with by a simple process of elimination. If a clicking noise is heard then where is it coming from? First, isolate the problem to the keys or the action. Activate the lever with your fingers but keep the key still. If no click is heard then the problem is the key. Raise the the lever away from the key and play the key. If all is silent then the clicking is somewhere in the action.

Ailment

'On clicks' (i.e. clicking occurs when the system is first set in motion)

Causes   *Remedies*

Keys

1.	Foreign object under key	Remove
2.	Front rail washer: missing	Fit new washer
3.	Capstan felt cap: missing. This click may not be heard with either of the isolating tests as there will be no contact between the key and the action	Fit new cap

Action

1.	Butt flange: loose or broken	Tighten or replace

2. Hammer shank: loose, either at the hammer or butt end. Check by trying for movement of the hammer with your fingers — Remove and re-glue

3. Back stop shank: loose, at the stop or butt end — Remove and re-glue

4. Tape: too far to the right and hitting adjacent section — Adjust

Ailment

'Off Clicks' (i.e. the clicking occurs as the system comes to rest)

Causes	*Remedies*

Keys

1. Backtouch (the strip of felt on the keybed at the rear end of the keys): worn — Replace with a strip of felt of the same thickness. Start at one end, gluing (with a white glue) as you go, and pull the felt out a little as you go to avoid wrinkling. Meticulous gluing is not necessary, just use enough to hold the strip in place. If the piano falls in the 'just something I bought cheap for my daughter to learn on. If she sticks at it I'll get her a better one next year' category of musical instrument, then just put a patch in

2. Nameboard felt (the narrow felt strip on the fallboard): missing or worn — Cut and glue a new length

Action

1. Notch felt: missing — Cut and fit a new piece. If there are many clicks caused by missing notch felts then a complete renewal may need to be carried out for the others are likely to break at any time

2. Hammer-rest rail felt: loose — If the felt is in good condition remove the rail and re-glue. If in poor condition then clean off the old felt completely and glue on a new strip, using white glue

3. Washer on the front wire assembly (overdamped): missing — Fit new washer

| 4. | Lever bushing (in the hole in the lever that takes the front wire assembly— overdamped action): missing | Fit a new piece. This is a tricky job as the hole is so small. Dry fit first: cutting slightly undersize will help |

Ailment

Pedal squeaks (sustaining pedal). Some pianos have such noisy pedal systems that one can be forgiven for thinking that they have their own built-in rhythm sections

Causes	*Remedies*
1. Pedal-foot rebate felt: missing	Re-felt
2. 'U' spring: not fixed to the bottom board by two screws	Place a felt pad underneath
3. Pedal hinge: corroded	Oil
4. Horizontal rods ('loud' and 'soft' on the left-hand side): rubbing against each other	Investigate and use common sense
5. Upright rod guide block: felt worn	Bush the hole in the block with a narrow gauge felt. If the design is such that there was no felt in the first place, and the rod is a tight fit, then there will be no room for new felt. In this case lubricate the touching parts with a finger of Vaseline (petroleum jelly) or household soap
6. Felt pad on top of upright rod: missing	Cut a new piece and glue into position. As a ready-made clamp hold down the damper-rail lift hinge with your left hand, depress the pedal with your right foot and hold this position for a few moments
7. Metal damper lift rod (situated at the back of the action): rust spots on hinges	Test by activating the action remaining in the piano with your fingers. To cure any squeaks, remove the action from the piano and apply a touch of oil to the hinges using an artist's brush

Ailment

'Sounding on'—overall. The piano insists on making music long after you have left it

Causes	*Remedies*
1. Adjusting nut (sustaining pedal): adjusted down too much, not allowing the dampers to be set firmly against the strings	Slacken until the top of the vertical rod is just below the damper lift hinge
2. Vertical rod (sustaining pedal): disconnected from the horizontal and jammed in the guide block hole	Investigate. The rod may need sanding at the point where it enters the guide block
3. Action securing nuts and clips: loose	Particularly check the sideclips and centre locking nut, just above the damper rail, as is usually found in overdamped actions

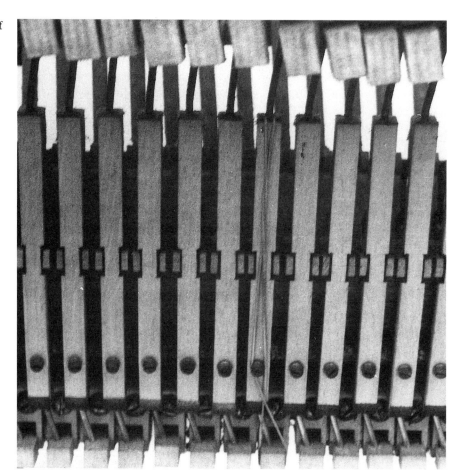

Figure 30. Cunning use of a rubber band

Ailment

'Sounding on'—individual. An individual note persists yet the rest are quiet

Causes	*Remedies*
1. Damper, or damper felt: missing	Replace
2. Damper: out of line and not effective on all the strings	Re-align
3. Damper: not set in close enough to the strings	Re-set
4. Damper spring (underdamped: worn or broken	This problem can be overcome speedily by using a rubber band as shown in Figure 30. This is not a very elaborate method but it is effective, and often used by tuners in a hurry
5. Front wire and damper rail flanges (overdamped): tight	A touch of piano action lubricant is needed
6. Front wire assembly (overdamped): bent	Straighten

Other noises

Ailment

'Twanging damper'—as the key is released and the damper returns to the strings a twanging noise is heard

Causes	*Remedies*
Either rusty strings have left a corrosive deposit on the damper felt or a sticky liquid; such as fruit drink, has been left on top of the piano (a nasty habit), and allowed to seep in	Pull the action forward away from the strings and clean the damper felt with a small piece of sandpaper and a wet finger. Careful squeezing with the fingers to break up the corrosion may be necessary. The strings, if they were the cause in the first place, should be cleaned with a dry cloth

Ailment

A dull thud—an unmusical sound which dies straight away even if the key is kept down

Causes

The damper is set too close to the strings. If many such sounds exist then the damper rail, especially in an overdamped action, is screwed in too tightly

Remedies

Adjust with the centre locking nut

Ailment

Vibrations

Causes

More often than not vibrations can be traced to the panels, lids, brass hinges or fixings

Remedies

Hold each piece firmly in turn and play until the offending part has been traced. If still without success then something may have fallen into the bottom of the piano, either in the front or between the soundboard and the backing cloth. See under 'Casework renovation' (pp. 124–5), as it may be necessary to remove the cloth

Ailment

Piano tone too quiet

Causes

For both underdamped and overdamped actions, check the vertical rod, soft pedal. It may have come away from the horizontal rod and jammed in the guide block. This will cause the hammer-rest rail (under-damped) to be forward, or the celeste rail (overdamped), to be risen

Remedies

Re-fit vertical rod

Overdamped only: the celeste rail may have jumped out of its slots

Re-fit celeste rail

If the problem cannot be traced to the soft pedal then the cause could be that the hammers are in a poor condition.

See under 'Toning' (pp. 114–18)

GRAND PIANOS

The causes and remedies of 'sticking' and 'clicking' are much the same as described for the upright. Some irritations experienced particularly with grands are given below.

Ailment

Play key and no resistance is felt and nothing seems to happen.

Causes	Remedies
Probably the loop cord has broken and the jack has no contact with the hammer roller	Look under 'Loop and wire' (p. 29)

Ailment

Several adjacent white keys stick

Causes	Remedies
Yes, it has been mentioned before, but this time it isn't the keyslip fouling the keys but the keys fouling the keyslip	Remove the keyslip and give the action a firm push home

Ailment

The key meets considerable resistance about half-way down and effort is required to overcome it. This problem is usually accompanied by a rubbing noise

Causes	Remedies
The cause is either with the jack's angle of contact with the roller or the roller itself	
1. Jack regulating screw	Adjust and test—this in itself can be a problem. The regulating screw has a spade, or flat end, and to turn it a tool has to be specially made with a slotted end and narrow enough to pass through the let-off dowels. A straight line connection between screw and tool is essential or the screw may snap. Alternatively, the unit can be detached and the screw turned by guess-work.

2. The leather on the roller may be grooved and roughened after years of punishment from the jack

To test if the roller is to blame, soften and re-shape with a wet finger. This may well improve the touch but don't jump for joy yet because the improvement is unlikely to last. The test might have confirmed the worst—the leather needs renewing. If the problem is present more or less throughout the entire range then a complete renewal is needed. Think hard before tackling this job yourself. Most grands have 88 of all parts and stripping out the old and fitting in the new is quite a task. If the piano is worth something then it may be wiser to pass this work on to an experienced technician.

Ailment

A damper sticks or returns slowly

Causes

Remedies

1. Flange: tight

Remove action and lubricate flange at the bottom of the damper wire

2. Damper wire: tight in guide rail hole

Depress pedal, hold down and brush corrosion from the wire in the area where it enters the hole

Ailment

Buzzing string

Causes

Remedies

Damper wire: touching string

Bend wire. This may need to be done from underneath

Ailment

Scuffing noise from rear of action

Causes

Remedies

Back check: in too close

Remove action and adjust

Ailment

Continual rattle when playing

Causes	*Remedies*
Foreign object, (often a ballpen) on the soundboard, hiding under the iron frame	Fish out with a rod

Ailment

Metallic sound from a hammer at a stringing break

Causes	*Remedies*
Hammer: out of line and hitting the underside of the iron frame	Take out action and re-align

Ailment

Severe up and down key wobble

Causes	*Remedies*
Back check: not catching hammer	Take out action and adjust check

Ailment

Pedal squeaks

Causes	*Remedies*
Could be one of many	Get underneath and tighten all fixing screws on the pedal lyre. If the pedal still squeaks lubricate the damper-lift rail dowel with a touch of Vaseline (petroleum jelly) or household soap. If you suspect the noise is coming from the pedal box then take off the entire trap work—it comes away quite easily—and place on a bench. The screws to open the box are underneath

Tuning

SUMMARY OF THE SCIENCE

The science of sound is a very extensive subject but only a little knowledge is necessary to help you to tune your piano.

Pitch

'Pitch' must be explained first. Over the past centuries pitch has varied a great deal, sometimes several pitches being in existence at the same time, in different parts of the world. Since 1939 pitch has been standardized and now stands at A49 = 440cps. (Don't get frightened!) For the sake of identification the notes on a piano are numbered from the bass, starting at A1. A49 is therefore the A above Middle C. 'CPS' stands for 'cycles per second', therefore, if the piano is on pitch, when A49 is played the strings vibrate 440 times per second.

This international standard, conveniently known as 'A440', is sometimes called the 'Orchestral A', and is a convenient, middle-of-the-range pitch to which strings, woodwind and brass can tune. The oboe is the usual 'pitchgiver', and the players tune their instruments to match this sound, the violinist, for instance, adjusts his 'Open A' string to be at the same pitch as the A of the oboe. When all this is done then the orchestra can play 'in tune' and 'on pitch'.

Calculation of frequencies

Any named note vibrates twice as fast when played an octave higher and, obviously, half as fast when played an octave lower. Simple mathematics will show that A61 = 880cps and A37 = 220cps. (These are the As above and below A49.) In order that all the semitones (the next key on a piano, up or down, black or white, to any given note) in between any given octave are at an equal distance apart, the cps of each ascending semitone is calculated by multiplying the cps of the semitone below by the twelfth root of two, or 1.0594631. (This is heady stuff. Read it then forget it. But there is a reason for its mention.)

A49 (440cps)	×	1.0594631	=	A sharp 50 (466.2cps)
A sharp 50 (466.2cps)	×	1.0594631	=	B51 (493.9cps)
B51 (493.9cps)	×	1.0594631	=	C52 (523.3cps).

C52 is the pitch of the piano tuner's tuning fork, to be dealt with later.

Equal temperament

An octave made up of equidistant semitones is known as being in 'equal temperament'. The only interval which is pure or 'beat-less' in a scale in equal temperament is the octave itself. All the other intervals produce a 'beat', and to produce the right amount of beating the intervals must be deliberately, but scientifically, mis-tuned. This is known as 'laying a scale', 'bearing', 'tempera-ment' or 'middle octave'; i.e. tuning to a point where all the semitones are of an equal distance apart. This is the aim of the piano tuner, and the reputation of a professional stands or falls on his level of accuracy when performing this task. But tuning by semitones to any degree of accuracy is impossible. A piano is tuned by 4th and 5ths and octaves, the octaves being tuned pure, and the 4ths and 5ths being mis-tuned, or tempered, from the pure.

A serious study of acoustic science is mercifully not necessary for the family piano tuner, so pushing pages of mathematical calculations to one side, it is sufficient to say that if all the 4ths and 5ths were tuned pure then the piano would be so out of tune with itself that only one or two keys of the twelve major and twelve minor keys would be playable, the rest being unacceptable to the human ear.

Introducing a slow beat to each of the 4ths and 5ths in the first (middle) octave to be tuned, i.e., laying the scale, will allow *all* the keys to be acceptable to the ear, the beats themselves being too slow to be annoying.

Piano tuning is a compromise and it is arriving at this compromise which places the piano tuner in a world of his own. The mysteries of his art will gradually unfold in this chapter. Read on.

Tempered intervals

The beat rates of the 4th and 5th intervals, in equal temperament, in the scale F33–F45, average 1 per second. These are the easiest to listen to, decide upon and adjust, so this is the octave used by all piano tuners when laying the scale. Beat rates get faster as the intervals ascend and slower as they descend, doubling, or halving as the case may be, at the octave. The beat rates in the high treble are so fast and those in the low bass so slow as to be unusable in laying the scale.

The beat rate of the 5th between F33 and C40 is 0.590 per second (calculated from standard pitch). The beat rate of the 4th between C40 and F45 is 1.180 per second. Nobody in the world can possibly judge 0.590 or 1.180 beats per second, and in practical piano tuning the beat rates of the 4ths and 5ths are rounded off and calculated over 5 seconds, the figures being about 3 beats per 5 seconds for the 5th (F33–C40), and 6 beats per 5 seconds for the 4th (C40–F45). These rounded-off figures may also prove to be difficult, so working on an average of 1 beat per second (to be explained later) is suggested and will produce an acceptable temperament.

Laying a scale in equal temperament is done by 4ths and 5ths only. The beat rates of the Major 3rds are too fast to count, for example, the beat rate of the Major 3rd between C40 and E44 is 10.38 beats per second, a fast ripple, so these intervals are not *directly tuned* but used as checks only. 4ths, tuned downwards only, are tempered, that is, 'sharpened' or 'widened' from the beatless pure to introduce a slow beat. 5ths, tuned upwards only, are tempered, that is, 'flattened' or 'narrowed' from the beatless pure to introduce a slow beat.

Old, neglected pianos may not be up to pitch, and therefore the beat rates in the middle octave, and in all the other octaves, will be a little slower than those of a piano on pitch. Laying the scale in the middle octave is laying the foundation on which the rest of the piano is tuned. A poorly laid scale will be mirrored in the remaining octaves, above and below, but if all the 4ths and 5ths in this temperament octave have been set to produce a slow beat then a good job has been done.

To sum up:

> Octaves—tune beatless.
> 4ths and 5ths—temper to produce a slow beat.
> Major 3rds (check only)—a fast ripple.

This concludes the summary of the science. It is important that you understand it so that you know what is happening when studying technique, i.e. the practical application of the theory, which follows.

TUNING AN UPRIGHT PIANO

Tuning lever technique

Figure 31 shows the types of tuning levers and hammers that are available and other tools used in piano tuning. The star lever **(1)**, with eight maximum positions, is considered the best, though the square pin lever **(2)**, with four maximum positions, is adequate. If the piano to be tuned has oblong pins then the hammer **(5)**, is the preferred tool. The oblong pin lever **(4)** has two positions, but in practice usually only one can be used, as the action gets in the way of the handle and even then the one available position may be at too awkward an angle for manipulation. Whatever you do, never use pliers, spanners or wrenches as these will damage the pins, and without a good grip tuning becomes impossible.

Figure 31. Piano tuning tools

Position

The lever should be placed in position on the pin at about 'one o'clock', as shown in Figure 32. If the lever is placed in a three or four o'clock position the tuning pin may be pulled downwards and loosened in the plank. Concentricity is the most important issue in lever technique, that is, the pin must be turned on its own centre, remaining concentric to its hole in the plank, and must not be pulled, bent or twisted sideways.

Figure 32. Correct position of lever

Figure 33. A good purchase is essential

Securing purchase

Never use a 'free hand'; some part of the arm or hand must secure purchase somewhere on the piano. Try writing your name without resting the side of the hand on the desk. A similar lack of control will be experienced when manipulating the lever if a free hand is used. Figure 33 shows the arm resting on top of the piano and the hand with a firm grip on the lever. The lever can now be *pushed* to the left and *pulled* to the right (the reverse for left-handed tuners); control and counter-movement being afforded by the purchase secured by the arm on top of the piano. Because pianos vary in size and shape (as do tuners) this particular position may be difficult to obtain, the only alternative being to use the fingers to find purchase, in which case a strong hand is essential. Adjust the position as follows:

1. To slacken the string. Place the index and middle fingers on top of the piano, wrap the other two fingers around the handle and bend the thumb under as shown in Figure 34. Push anti-clockwise with the thumb and counter and control the movement with the fingers.

Figure 34. Controlling with your fingers, anti-clockwise

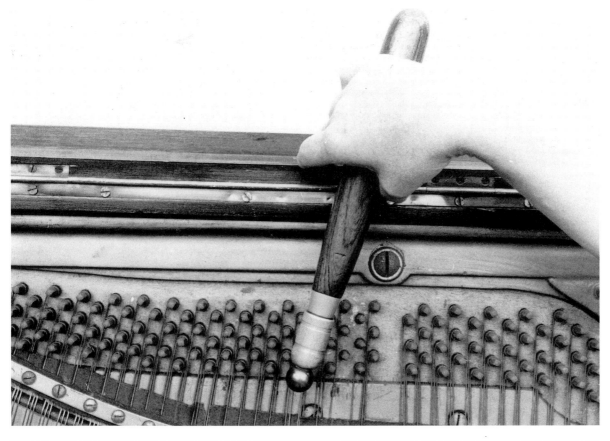

Figure 35. Controlling with your fingers, clockwise

2.   To tighten the string. Place the index and middle fingers on top of the piano and pull the lever clockwise with the other two fingers, the thumb extended along the handle to act as a counter and control.

Easing string tension

No matter what stage of tuning you have arrived at always lower the tension of the string before the final adjustment for the following reasons:

1.   Listening to the pitch being lowered as the pin is being turned will ensure that you are dealing with the correct string. If the lever is put on the wrong pin (and this can easily happen in the tri-chord section), when you pull up the string a frightening, deafening bang will ensure that you don't do it again.

2.   To release rust bonds which may have accumulated between the strings and bearing points.

3.   To give the string a chance to breathe and flex itself. After many years in the same position shallows and shoulders may have developed on the string at those points where it goes over and around bearing points.

Note: the amount a pin needs to be turned during normal tuning procedures is very small indeed. As an idea of how small, imagine the pin to be a clock face and any turns, either way, never being more than two or three minutes.

Exercises in lever technique

1. Depress Middle C to raise the damper and, using a Papp's wedge as shown in Figure 31, pluck the three strings to determine which is at the highest pitch. Assuming this is the one on the right, then its pin will be the lowest of the group of three in the plank. (If the piano has a celeste rail then remove it, as it gets in the way of the wedge.)

2. Place the wedge, in 'open' position between the left-hand string of Middle C and the right-hand string of B (the note below). This mutes the left-hand string of the C, allowing only the right-hand and middle strings to sound. Placing the wedge correctly in an overdamped action is like working in the dark and it may be necessary to pluck the strings, and position by sound rather than sight.

Figure 36. Placing the wedge in 'open' position

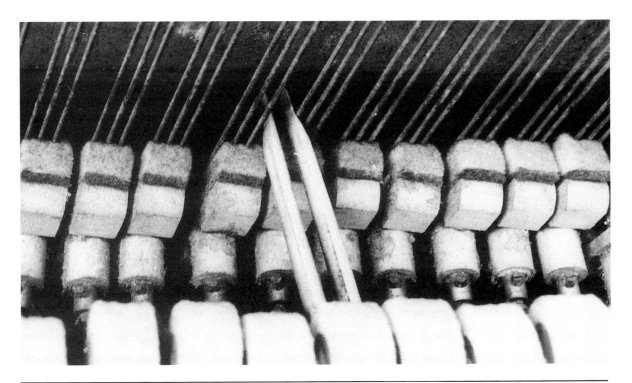

3.   Place the lever on the middle pin, making sure that it is fully on and at the one o'clock position.

4.   Play Middle C and keep the key depressed, as you need the note to continue to sound. Push the lever anti-clockwise with a smooth movement so as to slacken the tension a little and to lower the pitch, listening intently all the time and occasionally playing the key when the sound begins to fade. During this activity the pin and lever head must be kept in a straight line to ensure concentricity. The pin must be *turned on it's own centre* and not bent. Twisting the pin without actually turning it in the plank will lower the pitch temporarily but it will soon settle back to its original position. Whilst all this is being done (as if this isn't enough to be getting on with) listen intently as the pitch of the string lowers and you will become aware of the two strings gradually becoming more and more out of tune with one another.

5.   With the note sounding, pull the lever clockwise. This tightens the string and raises the pitch. Once again make sure to turn the pin on its own centre so that it remains concentric to the plank. As the pitch rises listen intently to the sounds of the two strings coming together. When they eventually merge together the sound becomes 'smooth'. Stop the movement there. Now remove the lever, taking care that the pin is not inadvertently given a backward turn.

Listening for beats

If the last exercises were done properly then the right hand and middle strings will now be 'in unison', 'smooth' or 'beatless'. That is how it should be with unisons. But deliberately mis-tuning unisons is a good way of learning how to listen for beats.

1.   With the wedge in open position, and the lever at one o'clock as before, play Middle C and listen once again to the smooth sound which you have just made. Play again, and with the sound maintained, slowly slacken off the middle string, just a little. Listen very intently and you will hear a quickening of beats as the two strings become more out of tune with each other.

2.   Play the key again, slowly turning the pin clockwise and concentrating on the sound, which will become less abrasive as the two strings approach unison. When the pitch of the string being turned is just a mere fraction away from that of the fixed string then a slow pulse will be sensed. This is the type of sound you must train yourself to listen for in readiness for tuning 4ths and 5ths, for when these intervals are properly tempered then a gentle pulse, or slow beat, will be introduced.

Note: do not spend too much time on one string as the pin may become loose. Use another tri-chord in the same region, or if you know of a 'write-off' piano then practise on that.

Setting the pin and string

If the string has been merely pulled up to pitch as in the foregoing exercises then a few days of playing will soon put it back out of tune. A piano in reasonable condition and surroundings should stay in tune for several months if has been 'solidly' tuned. This means setting the pins and strings.

A tuning pin is under stress in two ways: the tensional, downward pull of the string, which is considerable—70kg (160lb) or more—and the torsional strain, that is the coils of the string trying to unwind it. To counteract this, turn the pin ever so slightly sharp of its desired position and gently ease back.

A piano string goes around and over many parts between the hitch pin (at the bottom of the iron frame) and the tuning pin. The 'speaking' length (the section that the hammer strikes) is somewhere in the middle of these twists and turns. A string may 'hang on' to any of these bearing points, perhaps through rust or because of shallows and shoulders, so that only that section of string above that particular point is affected when the pin is adjusted. A few days of playing will distribute the tension evenly throughout all the sections, putting the string out of tune. To avoid this, raise the string to slightly over pitch and even out the tension by several solid taps on the key. Piano tuning should be a noisy business. If your tuning sends people gently to sleep then you are not doing the job properly. In practice, both activities of setting the pin and string are carried out at the same time.

Tuning unisons

1. Choose another tri-chord (to give Middle C a rest) in the middle region of the piano and, using the wedge, pluck the three strings to determine which is at the highest pitch, the other two strings to be tuned to this.

2. Place the wedge in open position, play the key and, with the note sounding, lower the pitch of the middle string, listening intently all the time and making sure that the pin turns concentrically in the plank.

3. Keep the sound going and raise the pitch until just slightly sharp of the fixed string.

4. Gently ease back to eliminate any twist in the pin and tap the key firmly several times to distribute the string tension, adjusting with the lever until a perfect, beatless unison is reached.

5. Remove the wedge and put to one side.

6. Lower the pitch of the third string.

7. Raise the pitch of the third string to a fraction above that of the other two. Set the pin and string as before and if a smooth unison is the result then you certainly have made progress in piano tuning.

Tuning octaves

1. Complete the unison of Middle C.

Figure 37. The wedge in 'closed' position

2. Place the wedge in closed position between the strings of C52 so that only the right-hand string sounds.

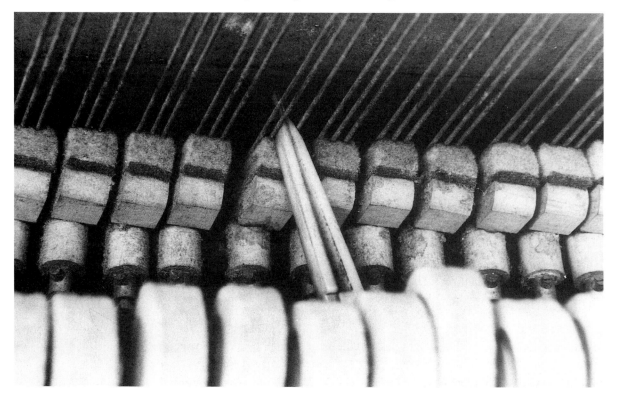

3. Play the two Cs together firmly, keep the notes sounding to determine whether the isolated string of C52 is sharp, flat or on the octave with Middle C. If in doubt—and remember, always play safe—then ease the tension of the string, and if the beats get faster as the pitch is being lowered then the string is flat of the octave with Middle C.

4. Raise the pitch, remembering the sound must be maintained. Turn (do not twist) the pin and set the pin and string until a beatless octave has been obtained. It will sound something like a smooth unison.

5. Tune the other two strings so that the tri-chord is in perfect unison and make your work last by setting the pins and the strings.

'Listen intently', 'Keep the note sounding', 'Turn the pin, not twist', 'Set the pin and string' have all been repeated deliberately in the preceding exercises and any further mention should not now be necessary. Every pin and every string, whatever stage of tuning you are at, should be dealt with in this manner.

Laying the scale

Having an ability with tools is fine for action repairs but this in itself is not enough for piano tuning. A musical ear, calm temperament, patience and a good manipulative technique are also necessary. Piano tuning is the most difficult aspect of piano servicing and laying a scale in equal temperament is the most difficult aspect of piano tuning.

Assessing the situation

This means: using the standard tuning fork which sounds at C52 and estimating the general level of pitch throughout the piano; and if noticeably below by how much you dare raise it, if you raise it at all. (When not in use the tuning fork should be wrapped in a soft cloth and put safely away.) If well below pitch then the factors to be considered are the age, type of iron frame, state of the strings and the general condition of the piano. Should the piano be very old (perhaps 70 years or more), not have a full iron frame (i.e. there is no iron plate covering the tuning pin plank) the general condition poor and the strings badly corroded and at breaking point, then tuning, the first time at least, is best done at the average overall pitch at which it stands. If the piano is in a robust condition with clean, healthy looking strings and just a whisker away from standard pitch then it can be brought up to pitch during its first tuning.

An old, neglected piano may be several semitones under pitch and usually in a case such as this the copper-wound bass strings will not have dropped in pitch as much as the all-steel treble strings. Common sense must prevail, which may mean lowering the bass strings somewhat. (Raising the pitch is dealt with later.)

Muting

The equal temperament octave is laid using one string only from each tri-chord, the unisons being put in last. Papp's wedges can be used, three being a convenient number as any more will cause crowding. With the wedge in closed position, mute the middle and side string of each tri-chord as you come to it, leaving only one string to sound. Keep just to one side, e.g. all the right-hand strings of the tri-chords in the octave. Seasonal changes will cause expansion or contraction of the wooden tuning-pin plank resulting in a kind of uniformity in the way in which the unisons are out of tune with themselves, i.e. the effect of expansion or contraction is greater on the top pin (because more wood is involved) than on the bottom pin. Pluck a few tri-chords and the pattern will identify itself. Lay the scale using the strings on the one side which are generally at a higher level of pitch.

Alternatively, muting can be done by using a felt or rubber strip to silence all the outside strings, leaving only the middle strings to sound. This method allows the complete octave (and a little more each side), as used in Method 1 (pp. 78–9), to be tuned without having to shift wedges. The action will need to be removed and the strip mute placed in between the strings by being carefully pressed in with a plastic or wood strip. Once the scale has been laid remove the strip and complete the unisons using a wedge.

Figure 38. Inserting the strip mute

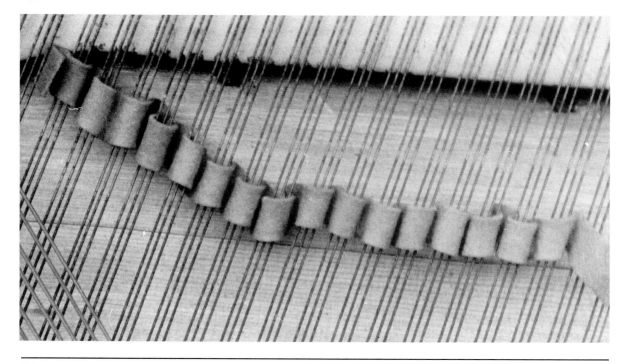

Training the ear

'Perfect pitch', usually associated with musicians and piano tuners and regarded by many as being a gift from the gods is a fine asset for piano tuning, though not absolutely necessary. However, a sense of interval distance is a must. From a given note it is essential that you can accurately pitch (aloud or inwardly) the notes an octave higher and lower, the 5th higher and the 4th lower. If you are unable to do this then you are advised to forget about piano tuning for a while until you have developed a reasonable musical ear. If you do not understand the basic rudiments of music then, with the help of someone who does, and who ideally has a piano in a good state of tune, an understanding of the very simple musical notation knowledge which is necessary for piano tuning will be made easy.

Musical illustration 1 uses white keys only, with C40 and C52 written in. The familar sound of tonic solfa is also written in between these Cs. Should the tonic solfa start on any key other than a C, then it would sound quite strange unless one or more black keys were used.

Musical illustration 1

DOH-RAY-ME-FAH-SOH-LAH-TE-DOH

C40   C52

Exercises

1. Starting from C40 learn to sing, or whistle, inwardly or outwardly (with a little prompting from the piano if necessary), the tonic solfa scale, ascending and descending as shown.

2. Play C40 only and practise pitching to C52, the octave above: 'Doh—Doh'.

3. Play C52 only and practise pitching to C40, the octave below: 'Doh—Doh'.

4. Starting from C40, sing 'Doh—Ray—Me—Fah—Soh'. Check your 'Soh' with G47 on the piano.

5. Play C40 only and pitch G47, the 5th above: 'Doh—Soh'. Check with the G.

6. Starting from C40 sing 'Doh—Te—Lah—Soh'. Check with G35 on the piano.

7. Play C40 and pitch G35, the 4th below: 'Doh—Soh'. Check with the G.

Still using the assistance of your musical friend if need be, practise the same exercises in different keys, which only means using different starting points. Keep to the central regions of the piano and with a little endeavour you will soon gain a feel for the interval distances of octaves, 4ths and 5ths.

About sharps (♯) and flats (♭)

To complete the theory necessary to understand the notation of the tuning methods (to be shown later) the use of sharps and flats must be explained:

- A sharp raises the pitch of a note by a semitone.
- A flat lowers the pitch of a note by a semitone.
- The five black keys can be indicated by sharps or flats and they are:

$$F\sharp = G\flat$$
$$G\sharp = A\flat$$
$$A\sharp = B\flat$$
$$C\sharp = D\flat$$
$$D\sharp = E\flat$$

Although the notation in the tuning methods could be written using only sharps or only flats, the reason for using both is that certain keys and chords are more familiar to a person who understands musical notation if written in the same manner as found in the writing of music generally. For example, C♯ in the Major 3rd check, stage 18, Method 1 (p. 79), with the A, is in keeping with the sharps as written when using the key of A Major. D♭ (the same black key as C♯) is the keynote of the Major 3rd check with the F, stage 30, Method 1 (p. 79), the key of D♭ Major being indicated by the use of flats. This will be further explained in the commentary accompanying the Methods.

Counting seconds

The beat rates of the direct tuning intervals in the equal-tempered scale are calculated in seconds, and for practical purposes rounded off over five seconds. Practise counting seconds by saying, at the usual speaking speed: 'a thousand and one, a thousand and two, a thousand and three', etc., and check with the second hand of a clock for accuracy. Adjust your speed if not in time and practise, without looking at the clock, until eventually (it may only take a few days) testing will show that you can keep good time over periods such as 20 or 30 seconds. Then practise in five-second measures, waving the hand with each second as if conducting, and imagine a gentle pulse, about one beat per second, in your head.

The Major 3rd Trap

Although it is an advantage for a tuner to be musical, it must be understood that a piano must be tuned scientifically and not musically. Falling into the Major 3rd trap will cause all kinds of problems. A Major 3rd sounds sweeter to the ear if tuned flat from its correct mathematical position in a scale of equal temperament. In order that all the semitones in the scale are of an equal distance apart, the Major 3rd should be sharp of the pure and the beating so rapid so as to produce a fast ripple. Do not directly adjust Major 3rds. If they are wrong, then start again, and find the errors in the direct tuning intervals of 4ths, 5ths and octaves.

Tempering intervals

Tempering is the art of listening to the two sounds of direct tuning intervals and adjusting those intervals until a slow beat is heard.

Tempering 5ths

Tune upwards only, that is, the upper note should be tuned to the fixed lower note. Put into a pure, beatless state as in 'Doh—Soh', tonic solfa exercise no. 5 (p. 75). Temper (i.e. flatten or narrow the interval) by gently easing back with the tuning lever until a slow beat is heard.

Tempering 4ths

Tune downwards only, to tune the lower note to the fixed upper. First put into a pure, beatless state with the aid of tonic solfa exercise no. 7, 'Doh—Soh'. Gently ease back with the lever and temper (in this case sharpen or widen) until a slow beat is heard.

Remember to keep the two notes sounding, turn concentrically and set the pin and string. Do not tickle the keys but play firmly, the two keys in use being depressed at the same time. Evaluate the pulse over five seconds.

In brief

1. Assess the situation, pitch, strings etc. If, after careful consideration of the condition, it is decided that the piano, on this occasion at least, is best tuned below standard pitch then stages 1 and 2 of the methods described below (using the tuning fork) will not be necessary.

2. Use correct lever technique at all times.

3. Play the note being tuned firmly and keep it sounding.

4. Unisons and octaves—smooth.
4ths and 5ths—a slow beat.
Major 3rds—a fast ripple (check interval only).

5. If you are 'tone-deaf' then leave the piano alone and find another interest.

The methods

Laying a perfect scale in equal temperament is a work of art and can only be done by a professional piano tuner who performs this task every day of his working life—and gets paid for it. Such perfection cannot be expected when tuning your own piano at home, but a satisfactory result can be obtained if all the advice so far offered in this chapter has been followed. The 'calm and patience' which has been mentioned before means, in practice, a willingness to return to the beginning and start again should errors creep in for, whatever errors are made in this middle, temperament octave will—if not corrected—be projected throughout the entire piano.

In the methods which follow the fixed note is indicated by a crochet ♩ and the note to be tuned indicated by a semibreve ○. Two superimposed semibreves, 𝆰 indicate the Major 3rd check intervals.

Method 1 (5ths and octaves)

This method eliminates the necessity for tempering downward 4ths, which some people find difficult. However, it also covers from F33 to B51 i.e. more than one octave and, having more direct tuning intervals in the stages (indicated by bar lines), may create more errors. (*See* Musical illustration 2.)

With the stages other than 'check stages' the tuning lever is used to adjust the tension of the string to be tuned to produce a slow beat with the fixed string. The lever is not used in the check stages, (Major 3rds), but the two notes are sounded together and a fast ripple indicates that the procedure, so far, has been carried out correctly.

C52, stage 1, is tuned directly from the tuning fork. Sound the note, tap the fork to make it vibrate and hold to the ear. Tune to a perfect unison. Continue tuning, as directed by the illustration, i.e. pure octaves and tempered 5ths, until arriving at the first check interval, stage 9. Listen for a fast ripple, about 10 beats per second, when the two notes are sounded together. The Major 3rd check interval, G—B, stage 11, should produce quite a fast ripple, about 16 beats per second. The G—B Major 3rd check in stage 13, being an octave lower, should produce a much slower ripple, in fact, half the speed. Continue tuning by 5th and octaves and Major 3rd checks step-by-step. From stage 19 onwards flats are used in the notation but to make check stages 20 and 24 easier to read, and in keeping with normal musical notation, sharps are employed. Stage 32 completes the octave F33—F45. Should the F33 and C40 result in a pleasing tempered 5th then you have performed a miracle. The unisons of this octave can now be put in and the rest of the piano can be tuned, as explained later.

Musical illustration 2

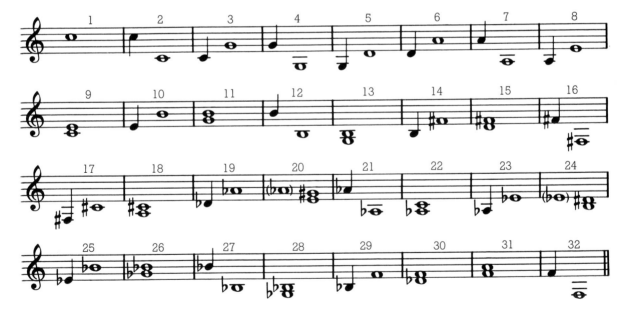

Method 2

This is a compact method and one which does not stray outside the octave. It is used by piano tuners internationally. (*See* Musical illustration 3.)

Tune C52 from the fork, and C40 from C52 as a beatless octave. Continue with downward 4ths and upward 5ths, testing for accuracy with the Major 3rd checks as indicated in the illustration. In order that the method can be contained within the F33–F45 octave, two consecutive downward 4ths are used, stages 8 and 10. If the fourth, stage 21, meets the requirements of a well tempered 4th then stand up and take a bow. Complete the octave, stage 22.

Musical illustration 3

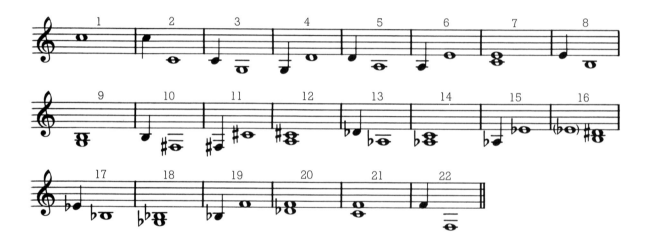

The rest of the piano

The rest of the piano is tuned from the tempered scale by octaves, e.g. E44—E32, E♭43—E♭31 downwards, F♯34—F♯46, G35—G47 upwards and so on. Either the bass or the treble can be completed first, or you may prefer a general 'fanning-out' of each side. If the piano is very badly out of tune then a quick, rough tune is advised followed by a fine tune, as pianos that are way out of tune will not remain in tune for long after just one tuning operation. If (because the piano is in a generally poor condition) a decision had been made to lower the bass strings a little then do this first. This should be done quickly to even out overall string tension on the framework and then a normal tuning should follow. Should the piano be in a generally good condition and the state of tune consistent throughout, but below standard pitch, you may decide (when laying the scale) that its first tune should be done at its existing, average level. In this case, as you progress with the tuning, assess the situation to decide how much, if at all, the pitch should be raised the next time it is tuned.

Possible problems

1. Inharmonicity. This problem usually occurs in the middle and treble regions of small pianos, because of the shorter, and therefore comparatively thicker, strings used. The family piano tuner is thankfully spared from the findings of physicists when explaining the cause of this problem; for the purpose of practical piano tuning 'inharmonicity'—a show-off word if ever there was one—means that when an octave is tuned correctly it will be out of tune with the other intervals. If put in tune with the other intervals then the octave itself will be out of tune. The only solution is a sensible compromise. Adjust as best as possible so that the octave is agreeable in some degree both with itself and with the other intervals.

2. False strings. A single piano string, when sounded, should produce one smooth, beatless sound. Now and again a string which has been either overstretched at a previous tuning, or wound on with a twist, will produce a beat of its own, causing ·confusion when you tune it to unison. Such a string, even when put into perfect unison with its two partners, will produce an out-of-tune sound when its key is played yet, oddly enough, if you deliberately put it slightly out of unison, it may produce a more pleasing sound. Once more, it is a case of doing your best and leaving the note at its most agreeable.

3. Break in stringing. The two breaks in stringing are necessary so as to allow the strings to pass either side of the upright supporting members of the iron frame. The lower break usually occurs at about D30 and the upper at about F57. The upper break causes the most tuning problems, one or two notes either side of the break having dull, short sounds and not the ringing quality as in the rest of the piano. This is an in-built design problem to be found in many vertical-strung pianos of the cheaper range. When tuning, there is nothing you can do about the matter other than your best.

4. A particularly flat note. Sometimes a note is considerably down in pitch compared with the general level. Coax each string up in turn, a little at a time, before starting the normal tuning procedure.

Tuning the bass

The copper-wound bass strings may produce a thick, woolly sound, and setting the octaves to a crisp, all-steel tempered octave can sometimes be difficult. Play the two keys firmly and check the note being tuned with 3rds, 5ths and 10ths, a 10th being an octave plus a 3rd, e.g. C28—E44. Always be willing to compromise, and leave the strings at a pitch where they are generally most pleasing with all intervals. Complete the unisons as you go.

The bottom octave, which uses only one very thick string per note, can often be quite fuzzy and deciding what is in tune or out of tune quite difficult. Those who can play the piano should make use of arpeggios, played slowly, then, by listening intently, adjust accordingly.

Tuning the treble

As you progress, tuning the treble by octaves from the tempered scale, then arriving at C52 will enable you to make a further check on any errors which may have been made when laying the scale. If the scale should prove to be at fault you then must take the decision as to whether you should re-lay it, for to continue tuning when you know it to be wrong is foolish. To check this octave take note of the following paragraph.

Tuning the first note in the treble, F♯46 (if Method 2 [p. 80] was used): as well as being put into a perfect octave, it must also stand the test with the D below, a Major 3rd, and the B below, a 5th. The second note to be tuned, G47, should be correct as the upper note of the octave, produce a fast ripple with the E♭ below and a slow beat with the C40. Similarly, all the ascending semitones to be tuned must agree with their related intervals. If you have to keep on sharpening or flattening octaves in order to squeeze them into some sort of order with the other intervals then you will soon run into a mess; for example, to flatten G47 to 'fit' the E♭ below, a Major 3rd, will put the G noticeably flat with the B above, another Major 3rd.

The top octave

The top octave is traditionally tuned a little sharp of the pure to give it an added brilliance which is particularly pleasing to pianists when playing ascending arpeggios into the higher reaches. Hints on tuning are given below.

1. Very little turning of the pin is required in order to make a considerable change in pitch.

2. The lever cannot always be placed in the one o'clock position. Place it so that you are comfortable *and* have control, perhaps at ten or eleven o'clock. Secure purchase with your forearm resting on top of the side panel.

3. It can be difficult to reach a final decision on the octaves and unisons. Plucking the strings with the wedge will help.

4. The short, thin strings used in the top octave have a rapid sound decay. Play the keys repeatedly and firmly to maintain the sound.

Raising the pitch

1. A very old piano in a very poor condition and several semitones under pitch will never see standard pitch again. A rise in pitch to within sensible safety limits is all that can be expected.

2. A piano in good condition and within sight of standard pitch can be brought up to pitch, even though it may take a few attempts. Whatever the situation, a number of tunings is advised. This is not only safer for the strings but is also necessary so that the sound board and all strain-bearing parts of the piano can be gradually introduced to the increase in tension as the strings are tightened.

3. The strain on the load-bearing framework is increased faster by turning the pins of strings that are very close to pitch than by turning the pins (the same distance) of strings that are well below pitch.

4. The more a piano string is tightened the more it is likely to resist and slip back to its previous position; this is another reason why a gradual increase, by several operations, is advised.

5. The copper-wound bass strings usually do not drop in pitch as much as the all-steel treble strings.

The procedure for raising the pitch

Always work fast when raising the pitch, so as to distribute an even increase in tension across the piano as quickly as possible.

Be prepared to lower your sights if you chose too ambitious a level in the first place and never raise the pitch and fine tune at the same time. The unisons and octaves need not be set perfectly when raising the pitch.

The following 10 stages should take half an hour or less and should be done in this order:

1. Take the C fork and compare it randomly with the other notes to estimate the general level of pitch. If the fork and C52 are nowhere near compatible then sound the fork with C♯53, or D54, and so on, until a degree of compatibility is evident.

2. A critical decision now has to be made: by how much should the pitch be risen at the first attempt? The best advice is just a little. This will mean more operations but is safer in the long run.

3. Raise Middle C, including the unisons, to what is considered to be a sensible level of pitch under the circumstances.

4. Quickly tune all the other Cs to Middle C, completing the unisons as you go.

5. Tune G47 from Middle C and then all the other Gs.

6. Tune D42 from the G and, without wasting time (so as to maintain your rapid, even distribution of tension) all the other Ds accordingly.

7. Continue in the same manner, laying a quick, approximate scale until every string in the piano has been risen. After this operation the piano will be in only a rough state of tune, but the increased tension will have been quickly and evenly distributed throughout the framework.

8. Play the piano firmly for a day or two so as to deliberately 'set the strings' and help to settle the pitch to its true level, which may well put it even more out of tune. Practising scales in octaves is good for this.

9. If it is still below pitch then, making use of the information gained in the previous operation, re-assess the situation and decide by how much, if any, it can be risen again. If you decide to continue with pitch-raising then with every successive attempt begin by laying the scale a little more accurately, though speed will still be necessary.

10. When the piano is on pitch, or at the highest level considered feasible, fine tune, more than one tuning being needed.

TUNING A GRAND PIANO

This is more comfortable than tuning an upright because of the good purchase that is always available with your forearm resting on the lid drop. Papp's wedges are not really suitable when tuning a grand as they pop out when the keys are struck. Use felt or rubber wedges, and a lever position, as shown in Figure 39. For the rest of the procedure, carry on as for an upright piano.

Figure 39. Tuning a grand

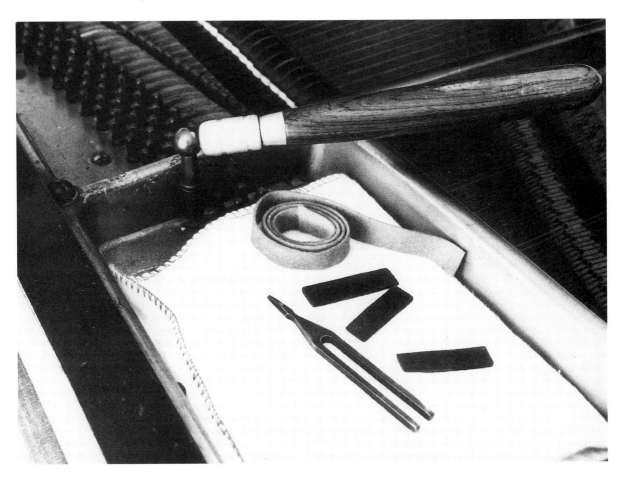

Problems with strings

UPRIGHT PIANOS

Treble strings

At first glance the all-steel treble strings appear to be of the same diameter, but in fact many different gauges are used when a

Figure 40. Coil lifter/ string spacer and brass wheel

piano is strung, the thinnest being used at the top then, after a few notes, the next gauge thicker is used, and so on. A typical scaling of the treble section may be: gauge 13 at the top, A85, gradually increasing by half sizes until the end of the section at about D♯31 where you are using gauge 19, each half-gauge increase being one thousandth of an inch. When replacing a missing or broken treble string a length of piano wire of the same gauge should be used. Never use a thicker gauge; it may well snap when approaching pitch. However, the next size thiner *can* be used and will not matter too much if you are working on a poor quality instrument. The diameter can be measured with either a micrometer or a wire gauge.

The two specialist tools required for fitting new strings—a combined coil lifter/string spacer and a brass wheel—are shown in Figure 40. The work can be done without the wheel but the lifter/spacer is indispensable.

Do not play a key if there are no strings for the hammer to hit, for this will put a strain on the hammer butt and flange. Always wear rubber gloves when handling strings, or wipe the strings with a clean, dry cloth after handling to avoid corrosion.

Fitting a double treble string

In most pianos the treble is strung using the system of one length of wire serving as two strings, the wire being wound on to a tuning pin, then passed around a hitch pin, and the other end then wound on to the next pin. Before you start, remove the action and a few keys from the area of the broken or missing strings. Should the new string to be fitted have to pass behind the copper-wound bass strings (as in the lower treble of an overstrung piano) some of these bass strings may have to be loosened so that your fingers can get in between and have room to work.

1. Cut away the loose pieces of broken string, being careful not to damage the listing (the coloured ribbon threaded through the strings).

2. Take a straight length of the broken string and measure its diameter.

3. Using the lever, turn both pins backwards by three complete turns, prising out the coils at the same time. Leave each pin with the hole in a vertical position.

4. Clean way any rust which may have gathered around the tuning pins, bridge pins and hitch pin and pass a piece of wire through the tuning-pin holes to ensure that they are clean.

5.   Using an extending metal rule, measure from the uppermost pin to the hitch, double this measurement and add about 25cm (10in.). This is a little longer than necessary and allows for any scoring of the ends to be cut off should pliers be used. Cut a length of the correct gauge wire.

6.   Thread the new length of string from underneath, i.e. passing under the pressure bar, if there is one, and over or under the listing as the case may be (check 'next door' to ascertain the arrangement). Feed through the hole in the left-hand tuning pin. To do this, you may need to use the lever and position the pin hole a little to the left or right. A piece of piano wire can be a stubborn beast and its angle of entry must be exact. (If it is not correct then it may peel, in which case you will see a thin strand of steel which means that the string has been weakened before you start.) Push it a little further through the hole so that there is enough for the fingers to handle, bend the end of the wire with a pair of pliers so that it is at a right-angle to itself and cut this piece off, leaving just a little of the bend so that the wire cannot slip back through the hole (Figure 41). If pliers were used to pull the wire through the hole then cut off the scored end before making the bend.

Figure 41. A small bend at the end of the wire

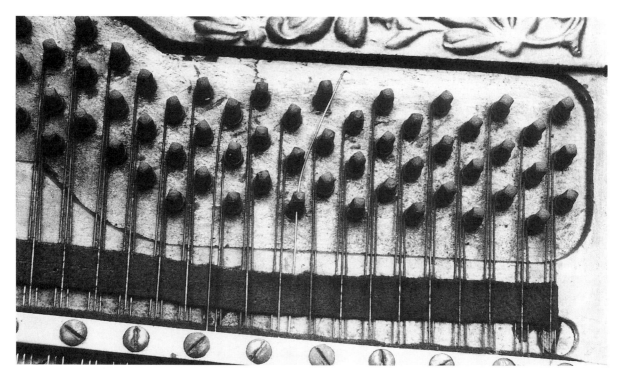

7.   Pull the wire down until it is checked by the bend you have left behind.

8.   Hold the wire taut with your left hand and wind the string on to the tuning pin for about two and a half turns (a tuning hammer is usually better for this activity than a lever), occasionally using the lifter to pull the coils towards you should they run astray (*see* Figure 42). Eventually (but not yet) you will need three neat coils, the wire touching all the way round but not riding on top of itself. If you release the tension with your left hand the coils may go all over the place. Once two and a half turns have been wound on then the coils should stay in position. They may open a little but can easily be brought back in with the lifter.

Figure 42. Using the coil lifter

9.   Making sure that the wire is not twisted, position in between the bridge pins (look at the others for correct arrangement) and pull taut around the hitch pin. Using pliers with protected jaws, squeeze together what are virtually now two strings at the point where the wire goes around the hitch, so as to leave a bend for the hitch. This also helps to keep the wire stable, making it easier for the next operation, and reduces the chance of twisting.

10.   The wire can now be taken off the hitch pin and again, making sure it is not twisted, thread the other end under the pressure bar and through the next tuning pin hole (*see* Figure 43).

Figure 43. Threading through the second pin

11. Fit the wire around the hitch, between both sets of bridge pins and pull up through the tuning pin until it is quite taut, adjusting the angle of the pin if necessary, to avoid peeling. If you use pliers to pull though, then grip the end of the wire as there will be excess to be cut off anyway.

12. Measure 7cm, (a little under 3in.) from the top of the tuning pin, bend it at right angles, and cut off, leaving a small bend as before. Pull the wire down until the small bend reaches the pin hole and stops any further movement. The wire will now have come away from the hitch and bridge pins.

13. With your left hand, hold taut what is now the right-hand string and wind on, using the lifter for neat coils. When about two coils are showing, place the wire into the correct position around the hitch pin and between the two sets of bridge pins. If the wire proves too tight to handle then slacken it a little. Wind on just a little more, until the wire springs into position and begins to look something like the others around it.

14. Using a screwdriver, press the wire firmly so that it is fitted safely around the hitch pin and bridge pins. Using a pair of pliers, preferably with the jaws covered by rubber sleeves, squeeze the two strings together as shown in Figure 44.

Figure 44. The wire must sit securely around the hitch

15. At the other end of the coil lifter there will be a string spacer. Put the two new strings into alignment with the existing string as shown in Figure 45.

Figure 45. Using the string spacer

16. Tighten each string just a little more, then 'wheel out' using the brass wheel to distribute the string tension evenly. (The wheel is used only on treble strings.)

Figure 46. Using the brass wheel

17. Using your fingernail, pluck the strings and gradually bring up each one until it is close to pitch. Plucking the strings a semitone below will act as a good guide. Remember to wipe each one with a clean, dry cloth after handling if you are not wearing rubber gloves.

18. Check that the wire is correctly in position at all the bearing points, the coils neat and the strings correctly spaced, then use the wheel once again with a firm pressure.

19. Replace the action and keys and tune up as normal (i.e. from the octave and using a wedge, each string gradually being risen in turn). Tune to slightly over pitch.

20. Check the pitch of the strings every few days and raise if necessary, until eventually all the kinks in the wire have been stretched out and the strings remain in tune.

Fitting a single treble string

Some pianos are strung with each tri-chord being made of one double and one single string. In order to fit a new single string

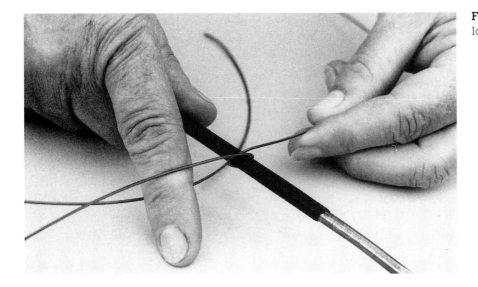

Figure 47. Starting the loop

you need a loop at one end of the length of wire. Commercially this is done with the aid of a machine but you can easily make a strong enough loop for repairing the family piano by using a screwdriver, or a large nail, and a pair of pliers. Bend the wire around the screwdriver, or similar tool, and start the loop as shown in Figure 47. Hold the wire with your right hand using a protected pair of pliers, and with your left-hand thumb bend the end of the wire around the main length until the required amount of coils have been laid. Cut off any waste. (*See* Figure 48.) Practise a few times with odd pieces of wire, laying coils on a screwdriver to improve your technique, before making a loop on the length of

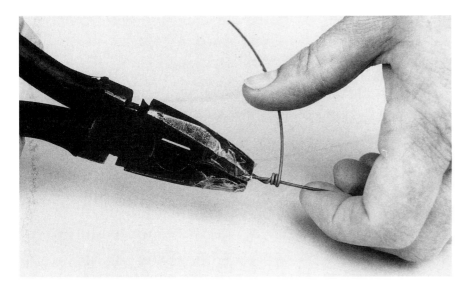

Figure 48. Laying on the coils

wire you actually intend to fit. Place the loop on the hitch pin and position around the bridge pins. Pull taut through the tuning-pin hole, measure 7cm (just under 3in.), make a bend and cut off. Fitting is done in a similar way to the previous instructions. Take special care that the loop fits snugly around the hitch. A single looped string can usually be fitted behind the bass section of an overstrung piano without having to loosen any strings.

Bass strings

Unlike the treble strings, the gradual increase in diameter of the inner cores and copper windings can readily be seen in the bass section. Fitting is as for the treble, but without wheeling of course. Because of the much heavier gauges, particularly in the deep bass, strong handling is required.

Broken bass string

A string rarely breaks in the middle of its length but rather at a bearing point and more often than not at the tuning pin. A string coiled tightly around a small diameter, such as round a tuning pin, expands on the outside and the combination of this and a deposit of rust produce its weakest point. Send the string to the stringmakers for them to make a replacement. If it is broken near the hitch pin fit the two parts together with sticking paper before sending them away or, if the loop is missing, ask for plenty of waste-end when ordering and make your own loop when the string is delivered. Before you make the loop place the string in position, the copper winding in line with its neighbours, and bend the wire around the hitch, or measure the distance between the hitch and winding.

Missing bass string (bi-chord)

Should a copper-wound string be missing from a bi-chord then you will have to allow for the difference in length measurement between the missing string and its partner, particularly in overstrung pianos, because of the staggered hitch pins and scaling of the iron frame. Using the strings either side as a guide, measure the distance between the hitch and the start of the copper winding, and also the length of the copper winding. Take the two diameters from the intact string and send this information to the stringmakers.

Missing single bass string (bottom octave)

Measure the lengths and diameters of the strings on either side.

Send off this information to the stringmakers and also state the position of the string, for example, if the missing string is the lowest C then put: 'the missing string is C4. Details enclosed are for B3 and C sharp5'. From this the stringmaker can calculate the scaling and produce a string of the right dimensions.

Note: When ordering a bass string giving the measurements only, i.e. without a pattern, always state 'when stretched', because stretching is considerable when a string is pulled up to pitch and, if there is too much winding, it may be drawn over the top of the plate.

Lifeless bass string

A bass string that when struck produces a dull thud instead of a musical sound probably has dust and dirt in the copper winding, which will reduce its vibrational qualities. Unwind the tuning-pin so that the string can be taken off its hitch pin, exercise the string by flexing and bending, clean with a stiff brush and re-fit.

Buzzing bass string

This is usually caused by the winding having come loose. Unwind the tuning-pin a little so that the string can be taken off the hitch, twist one turn (anti-clockwise) to tighten the winding, and re-fit.

Loose tuning-pins

Only about one third of a tuning pin can actually be seen, the remainder being fitted into a wooden wrest-plank, or pin-block, which has been specially manufactured using cross-banded laminations to withstand the enormous downward pull of the strings (about sixteen tons on a full-size piano at standard pitch).
  A plank can lose its grip on the pins locally or generally.

A local problem

Some of the reasons why one or more pins may be loose in the plank are listed below.

1. Somebody without any tuning-lever manipulative skill has tried to correct the pitch of an out-of-tune string without following the rules of concentricity, thereby widening the tuning-pin hole.

2. At the break in stringing, treble end, a bunch of six pins are crowded together and this in itself contributes to a weakness at this point. Because of the tuning difficulties (which have already been explained) which are encountered in this area an excess use of the lever may have occurred.

3. Some pianos with an overdamped action have been designed without much thought for the tuner, and the damper rail is set so high that the bottom row of pins is difficult for the lever or hammer to locate. Twisting and bending of the pins, thereby loosening them, is not unusual in this circumstance.

4. The pins on an old piano, even though the piano may have been expertly and regularly tuned, will eventually become loose simply because of the amount of tunings.

Dealing with a loose pin

Should just one or two pins be loose and the others a good fit then the correct way to deal with the problem is to fit an oversize pin. Unwind the pin with the lever and, with one hand free, pull the wire as it uncoils so as to get it as straight as possible. Once out of the pin hole attend to the string with protected pliers and try and squeeze out any bumps. Completely unwind the pin, and when out measure its diameter with a micrometer and select a new pin the next size larger—but preferably the same length as there are several lengths. Tap the new pin in flush with the others, checking with a straight edge such as a rule, then turn backwards by three turns. Fit the string and tune.

Bronze cylindrical bushes, split down the sides so that they can be adapted to fit any size pin hole, can be used. Unwind and take out the pin, tap the bushing in flush with the plank, tap in the pin and complete as described above for fitting an oversize pin.

If you are unable to get hold of new pins or bronze bushes then a speedy way to deal with the situation is to remove the pin and cut a bush from a small piece of sandpaper. Fit this around the pin and trim to size. Place the bush in the hole, rough side out, make sure it is properly seated and not overlapping and tap in the pin. Should the paper crinkle when fitting in the pin then pick it out with a hooked tool and try again with a new piece. Sometimes, using this method, the pin may be more successfully inserted by turning it in clockwise. When all is done fit the string and tune.

A pin that has been damaged by, say, using car engine tools instead of the proper equipment may be unable to receive a tuning lever, thus making tuning impossible. Try using a small file to re-shape the edges of the pin.

A general problem

A plank deteriorates with old age and as its natural oils dry out the pins become loose, making tuning unstable if not impossible.

Premature ageing of the plank can be caused by placing the piano against a radiator, which hastens the drying-out process.

Fitting a new plank is an immense undertaking and can only be carried out in a professional workshop by experts using specialist equipment. A brief description of the work follows.

The action and keybed are removed. The iron frame is removed and the old plank unbolted, de-glued and taken out. A new plank is made to pattern, which includes drilling 220 or more holes, each set at the angle of the original. The new plank is then fitted to the piano using hot glue and bolts. The iron frame, hooked to an overhead hoist, now has to be re-mounted, re-seated and bolted correctly. Next, the strings have to be wound on, and in many old pianos the original strings will be unusable and a new set will be needed, including the expensive copper-wound bass strings. Finally, the keybed and action are re-fitted, followed by several tunings. The cost for this operation? About half the price of a new piano.

Wipe away the tears, help is on the way . . .

Figure 49. Applying pin-block restorer with a syringe

Pin-block restorer

Pin-block restorer is a mixture of wood alcohol, glycerine and resin, and when applied to the plank it swells the wood, improving its grip on the pins. Application is simple and the results encouraging.

Lay the piano on its back (*see* 'Casework renovation' p. 123) and apply a few drops of the restorer around each pin using a medical syringe for good penetration as shown in Figure 49. Two small bottles should be plenty for a good dose. Leave the piano on its back for a week to allow the mixture to soak in well, then put it upright and tune.

A reprieve

Should the piano be in such a wretched condition that the above remedy is not worth the effort then before giving it a Viking funeral (set on fire and pushed out to sea) allow it a last chance by inserting felt wedges between the strings to mute the offending strings (*see* Figure 50). Unfortunately, fitting wedges in this way may mean that good strings are also muted and the more wedges that are used the more the instrument will take on the sound characteristics of a harpsichord. At least your Bach will sound authentic.

Finally, a plank problem and standard pitch do not go hand in hand. Tune at a level where there is a reasonable chance that the piano will stay in tune for a few months.

Figure 50. A 'last chance' with felt wedges

GRAND PIANOS

Imagine a grand to be an upright on its back and follow the instructions as given for the upright. A comforting thought—no bending and stretching—and no keybed in the way.

Note: Tapping in pins. If you wish to tap a tuning pin into a grand plank you must first remove the action and support the plank from underneath with a few wooden blocks wedged between the plank and the keybed. This is a safety precaution to prevent the plank from breaking. This safety precaution is not necessary with an upright piano as the plank is well protected by stout wooden back posts.

Regulating

When a new piano leaves the factory it is in a good state of regulation, that is, it has a positive sense of touch under the fingers and a positive response from the action. As the years pass, the felt washers and pads to be found in the keys and action gradually wear, usually unevenly, causing an uneven touch and response and an uneven appearance of the keys. Regulating, briefly, is adjusting so as to correct the irregularities caused by the wear.

A piano whose keys and action are totally out of regulation may

Figure 51. Regulating tools and materials

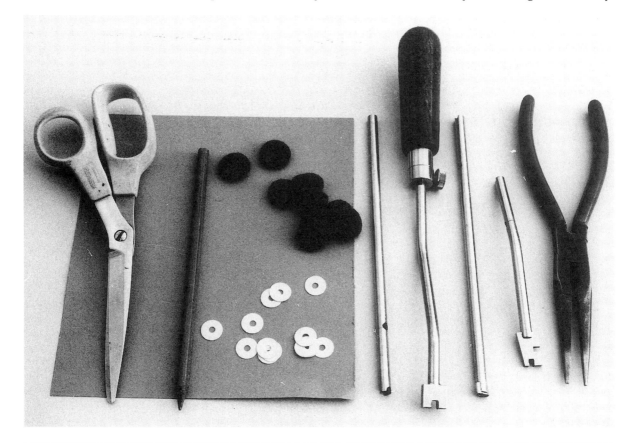

need a major regulating overhaul and this is done by following the standard mathematical formula which I have given in each case. A piano with a generally good touch and response but having just a few annoying defects here and there will only need a partial regulation, any offending part being brought into regulation by being lined up with an adjacent part in correct working order.

Although regulating is chiefly concerned with the 'to and fro' activities of the action, it is wise to check that the hammers, dampers, capstans and backchecks are in correct sideways alignment. Also put right any sticking or sluggish parts, as regulating is impossible unless the movements are free. These points have already been explained in 'Action repairs' (p. 20).

Do not regulate to precision measurements simply for the sake of it. If the touch and response are good, then leave well alone, even if they do not conform to the standard mathematical requirements.

A selection of items, some bought, some home-made, sufficient to do an adequate job, is shown in Figure 51.

UPRIGHT PIANOS

Levelling the white keys

A piano is played more in the middle than at the ends, so obviously there will be more wear in the central regions. A piano should show a good, even 'set of teeth'. A bow in the centre of the keyboard means that those keys in that area are out of regulation. Correct them using the following procedure.

1. Using thin, but stout cardboard, such as a business card, cut a piece about 50×25mm (2×1in.) and place between two white keys, either at the the high treble or low bass. Resting it squarely on the keyslip mark the height of the key on the cardboard as shown in Figure 52.

2. Using the cardboard, and its mark as a gauge, check the height of the white keys in the middle area of the piano and you may discover that they have sunk. If the keys have sunk but the bow is minute then leave well alone.

3. If the bow is considerable then remove the keys (marking their location on the balance rail in pencil) and put them to one side. Loosen the balance rail by slightly unscrewing the fixing screws, and insert a few pieces of cardboard packing underneath the centre of the balance rail to compensate for the bow; tighten back up. (*See* Figure 53.)

Figure 52. Marking the height of a white key

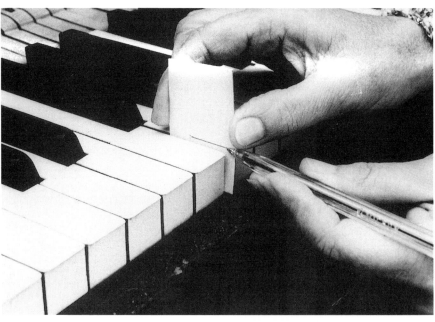

Figure 53. Packing up the balance rail

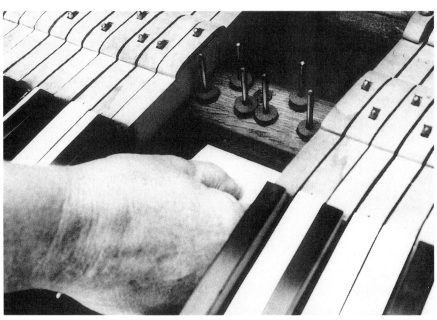

4. To check that sufficient height has been regained replace a few white keys in the middle area (following your pencil marks to ensure that they are properly re-located) and measure them against the cardboard gauge

Note: Forget about perfection when regulating a very old piano in poor condition. An improvement is all that should be expected.

Should only a few white keys here and there be below the general level then remove these keys and pack them up to height by fitting one or more paper washers underneath the balance-rail felt washers as shown in Figure 54. Keep the gauge, as it will be used later.

Figure 54. Inserting paper washers

Levelling the black keys

1. Any unevenness in the level of the sharps is not as visually obvious as with the white keys.

2. If packing was used at the balance rail to take out the bow and level the white keys then the black keys will have risen by the same amount, but could still be out of regulation.

3. Make another cardboard gauge, this time in the shape of a square arch, and lightly rest its legs on top of two white keys, either at the treble or the bass, straddling a black key. Make sure the white keys are not depressed.

4. Trim the feet of the arch with scissors until you have a good fit around the sharp. The black keys should ride about 12mm ($\frac{1}{2}$in.) above the white keys (*see* Figure 55).

5.   Use the gauge to check for any sharps which may have sunk, and pack up to height using paper washers underneath the felt washers on the balance rail. Keep the gauge for later use.

Figure 55. Marking the height of a sharp

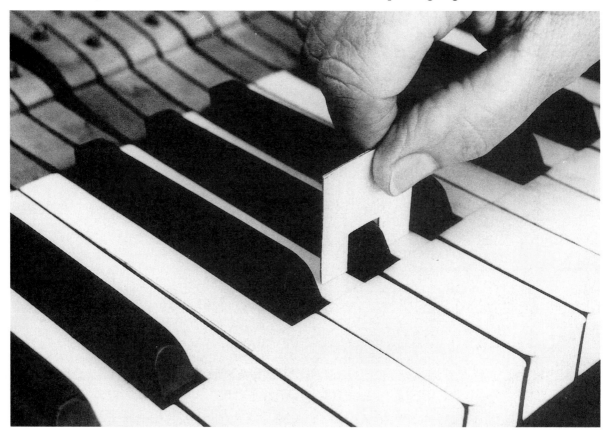

Key dip

Key dip is the distance a key travels from rest until stopped by the felt washer on the front-rail pin. The standard measurement is 10mm ($\frac{3}{8}$in.); this figure (and the others which follow later in this section) being adjudged as both mechanically efficient and satisfying the needs of the pianist. Avoid becoming obsessed with clinical accuracy when involved with a well-worn, old piano. If the dip is near the mark and the touch and response satisfactory then leave things as they are.

To check the dip of a white key mark the cardboard gauge you made for levelling with a line 10mm($\frac{3}{8}$in.) below the key-height mark and check the dip as shown in Figure 56. An incorrect key dip can be regulated at either the balance or the front rail, depending upon the cause. If the key is out of level then correcting by adding or removing paper washers at the balance rail will probably correct the dip. If the key is level then correcting the depth of dip at the balance rail will obviously throw the key out of level.

If the key height is correct and the dip too deep then either fit a new felt washer on the front-rail pin (as it may well be worn or missing) or pack up with paper washers.

If the dip is too shallow then correct by removing the paper washers, if any, or clean away any debris (the most likely cause) from around the front-rail pin.

The same principles as just described are used to check and correct the key dip of a sharp, using the arch-shaped gauge with a line drawn 10mm ($\frac{3}{8}$in.) below the key-height line. Measuring the dip of a black key will present a slight problem because of the bevelled front end. Use sensible judgement.

Figure 56. Checking the key dip

The capstan

A capstan is simply an adjustable extension of the key. Several designs are used, not all resembling a capstan (*see* Figure 57). Those of true 'capstan' shape, such as the common wooden dowel type **(1)** are adjusted in position with a long, pointed narrow rod. The rocker type **(2)** is also regulated whilst in position but using a screwdriver, slackening one screw and tightening the other, hence the rocking, as required. To adjust the last type **(3)** (only found on some old pianos) the key will need to be removed and the felt pulled back to expose the regulating screw.

When properly regulated the capstan will be in contact with the lever at the moment when the lever is risen to such a degree that the jack is just a fraction away from activating the hammer butt. To check this, 'tickle' the key and you should see a slight movement in the backcheck—no more than a quiver—but the hammer should remain still. This 'tickling' is a movement less than the thickness of a white key covering. When the key is further depressed the hammer should start to rise.

If the capstan is set too low then too much of the key's see-saw movement will be used up before the hammer section is brought into play. The butt, receiving a delayed blow, will cause the hammer to travel towards the strings at a reduced speed, resulting in a weak sound. If the capstan is set so high that the hammer is already in a forward position when at rest, then the jack will be tripped far too soon (this problem to be dealt with next) and the hammer will not receive enough punch to reach the strings.

Figure 57. Types of capstans

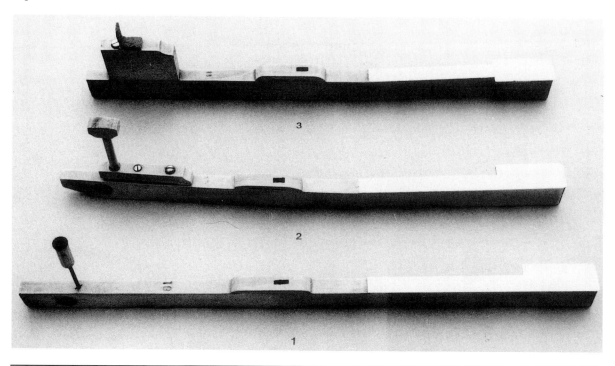

Hammer distance

The distance of the hammers from the strings, when at rest, should be about 45mm (1¾in.). Using a rule, take a few random measurements. If you are unhappy with the readings then check through the following list.

1. The hammer line is uniform but the distance from the strings is far too great (this will be accompanied by an overall sounding-on).

Check that the action is correctly seated and that the action bolts or clips are fitted securely. Check that the hammer-rest rail is secure.

2. One, or just a few hammers are too far back.

This occurs usually because the hammer is badly worn. Pack up with a felt pad, and then glue the pad underneath the rest-rail felt strip, or better still, fit a new hammer.

3. The hammer line is uniform but the distance from the strings is far too small.

The soft pedal may have jammed, causing the hammer-rest rail to be forward of its normal position.

Something may have fallen between the two sections of the rest rail (in an underdamped action) preventing them from closing together properly.

4. One, or just a few hammers are too far forward.

The capstan is probably set too high: adjust.

Let-off

One factor contributing to the distinctive quality of piano sound is the 'escapement'. Escapement is a term used to describe the way in which the lever section detaches itself from the hammer section just before the hammer makes contact with the strings. Completing the journey under its own steam, and helped by a spring-like length of shank, the hammer can now make a crisp rebound off the strings. The escapement, or 'let-off', is regulated by the let-off button and should happen when the hammer is about 3mm (⅛in.) away from the strings. If no escapement occurs, the continued contact between the two sections will not allow the hammer to rebound until the key is released, resulting in a dull thud. If the let-off happens much too soon then a lack of punch will produce a weak tone.

Depress the key very slowly and you will feel a sensation under your finger as the jack knuckle reaches the let-off button felt and the jack is tripped. The hammer will have moved forward towards the strings. Measure the distance from the tip of the hammer to the strings. If the light is poor, a piece of stiff, white cardboard with a well-defined ink mark drawn 3mm ($\frac{1}{8}$in.) from the one end will be useful.

If the above measurement is not met and, more importantly, the feel of the action is unsatisfactory, then regulate the let-off button, turning clockwise to make it trip sooner, as shown in Figure 58.

If it is only partially regulating, depress the two neighbouring keys using the hammer tails (the wooden parts nearest to you) as a guide, and bring into line by adjusting the let-off button.

Figure 58. Regulating the let-off button

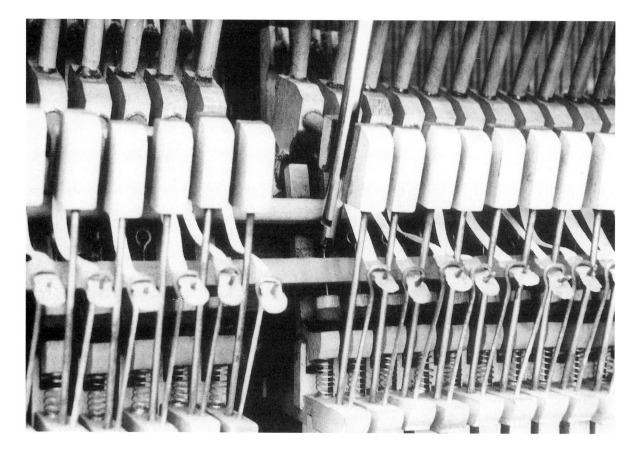

Useful tips

1. An overdamped piano may be best attended to with the damping system completely removed.

2. Let-off buttons must be turned concentrically, and you may need to remove the hammer-rest rail so that there is room for the regulating tool to be kept in a straight line with the button.

3. Be careful with old pianos, as corroded let-off buttons snap easily. If you suspect that this may happen then remove the button rail, treat each button with a drop of penetrating oil and leave overnight. Work loose with the fingers the next day.

Back check

The purpose of the back check is to control the hammer on its return. It should be in such a position as to check the catcher (back stop) after the hammer has travelled about a third of its return journey, that is, when it is approximately 15mm ($\frac{5}{8}$in.) away from the strings. If the check is in too close then it may engage with the catcher on the rise, stopping any further activity. If too far away then it will miss the catcher altogether and the hammer will bounce on the rest rail.

Play the key firmly and keep it depressed. Measure the distance between the hammer and the strings using a rule or a piece of stout cardboard with a 15mm ($\frac{5}{8}$in.) mark. If you need to make some adjustment, use the check-wire regulating tool as shown in Figure 59, holding the lever firmly with your other hand. The side of the tool is used for sideways alignment and the front

Figure 59. Using the check-wire regulating tool

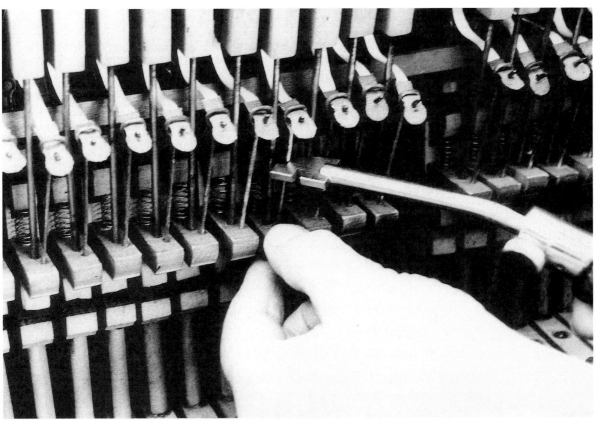

end for regulating. Bend at the bottom of the wire for general adjustment and at the top end for full surface contact with the catcher. Partial regulating is done by depressing a few keys at the same time and aligning the check with those around it.

Bridle tape

The tape should be adjusted so that there is just the slightest amount of slack when at rest. Too much slack and it will not assist in the hammer's return. If too tight then the jack, when rising, may not be able to free itself from the hammer butt. Adjustment of the bridle wire is easily carried out with the fingers.

Damper

The damper should start moving away from the strings when the hammer is about halfway through its outward journey. At this point of the activity the added weight caused by the resistance of the damper spring (underdamped action), or the front-wire assembly (overdamped action), will not be noticeable under your finger. Should the damper be late to move and brought suddenly into play at the same time as the escapement, then the combined weights may be evident under your finger, especially when playing gently.

The damper spoon (underdamped action) determines the start of the damper's movement. Depress a key slowly, study the system for a moment, and its principles will be easily understood. Holding the lever firmly with one hand, bend the spoon—closer to the damper lever if the damper is late to rise and away from the lever if rising too soon.

Though a special tool is available to adjust the spoon with the action still in position (as in underdamped actions), the home piano-tuner can do this job adequately by removing the action and adjusting the spoon with a pair of long-nose pliers.

Regulating the damper rise on an overdamped action can be done by any of the following methods.

1. Turning the wire button. The end of the wire will be threaded.

2. Fitting a felt washer underneath the button.

3. Bending, or straightening, the front wire. If this is done then ensure that the wire does not enter the hole in the lever at an angle.

At a glance

Some common, irksome problems that you can overcome speedily by regulating.

1. Blocking hammer: the let-off button is set too high.

2. Tamping hammer: the back check is too far away. If adjusting the check does not cure the problem then raise the capstan. If the capstan is set too low the jack will be short of its effective position but the jack spring will keep the knuckle at its normal position. The let-off will now occur too soon, causing the lever section to return to rest too quickly and the check to be out of position at the crucial time.

3. Sunken key (other than the balance-rail washer): if the capstan is set too low, or the felt top is missing then the key—if top heavy at the front—will sink below the line of the others.

4. Weak sound: check the key height; key dip; capstan and let-off.

Together, these items, if badly out of regulation (as is often the case in old pianos), will provide for a weak kick at the far end of the key and a lack of punch at the business end of the jack. This makes it necessary to thump in order to get some sort of response, the result being more black belts in piano playing than there are in karate.

A final reminder

An ancient piano (if you own a loop and wire type it will be older than your grandfather), if playing reasonably well, should be left alone. Brittle capstans which shatter, rusting buttons which snap, and tapes that crumble into little piles of dust before your very eyes can lead to nervous disorders!

GRAND PIANOS

Measurements, such as hammer to string distance, let-off, key dip and checking are as for the upright. Some aspects of regulating, exclusive to the grand, are given below.

1. Hammer distance
Place a marked piece of cardboard between the strings and hammers at the beginning and end of each break in stringing and check the distance. If the readings are at or near the mark, and the hammers in between each test pair complete a level line, then all is well in this department. Any hammer out of line can be adjusted

by the metal capstan. However, occasionally a tuner may deliberately have left a hammer a little out of line in order to overcome a malfunction in the action unit so, after adjusting, play the key and assess the situation.

2. Let-off
Check with a marked piece of card, choosing the beginnings and ends of stringing sections, and at random in between. Use your eyes to check for uniformity and adjust where needed by turning the let-off dowel.

3. Removing the action
Beware of any high hammers which may snap when the action is drawn out.

4. Repetition lever
Should be square under the hammer roller. If not, slacken the flange screw and correct with a paper shim. Also check the slot where the jack makes its entry. The top of the lever should be just above the top of the jack, by about the thickness of a piece of paper. The regulating screw is shown in Figure 25 (p. 43)

5. Jack
Should be roughly square to the centre of the roller. If it is too far forward (towards the hammer flange) it will produce a glancing blow which may not have the power to drive the hammer towards the strings; if too far back escapement may not occur. Correct with the jack regulating screw. (The problem of gaining access to the screw was described on p. 59.) Precise measurements to within a few thousandths of an inch are of little use for a well-used action so let your fingers and ears be the judges. Feel for resistance when the key is part-way down and listen for a rubbing noise.

6. Repetition lever spring
Rapid playing of the same key is the special feature of the grand's action; the key needs only to rise back up about half-way and the note can be sounded again whilst the hammer is in check position. The principle enabling this to happen is known as 'double escapement' and is the most notable improvement made on the piano's action since the piano first came to life in the early 1700s. Since its invention in the 1820s, double escapement has been the subject of intensive scientific research by the world's leading piano manufacturers; improvements and refinements forever being sought. The complexities of the principle can be left to the scientists to sort out. What follows is but a nutshell explanation.

As the key goes down the jack rises to send the hammer on its way, then the let-off trips the jack, knocking it out of position. The hammer strikes the strings, rebounds, and settles on the back check. As the key rises, the back check loses its hold on the hammer. The repetition lever, sensing that the pianist will strike again when the key is barely half-way up will not want to see the hammer fall back as far as the hammer-rest rail. Urged on by the tension of the repetition lever spring it dutifully steps in and supports the hammer in mid-air, just long enough for the jack to pop back in position and drive the hammer upwards again. And on and on the cycle goes, prestissimo, until someone turns the page.

A virtuoso performance all round, but it doesn't work if the spring is weak. The tension regulating screw is shown in Figure 25 (p. 43).

7. Hammer drop

Depress the key slowly and watch the hammer rise. When the jack is tripped the hammer rise is checked and resistance felt in the finger. The hammer should now drop back a little, the drop being no more than the thickness of a pencil mark. The adjusting screw is shown in Figure 25 (p. 43).

8. Back checks

Use the regulating tool, as explained for the upright (p. 109).

9. Damping

The lift and drop of an individual damper can be regulated by the screw on the damper-wire lever inside the piano.

When the pedal is used, the overall rise and fall is controlled by the pitman, which activates the damper-lift rail. If the lift is insufficient or the return to damp ineffective, crawl under the piano and investigate. The pitman is mounted on top of a straightforward leverage system. Operate the pedal by hand and assess the situation. The regulating screw is in the lever. Tighten to increase lift and slacken if the dampers are set too high. It is possible that an unsatisfactory return to damp is not due to faulty regulation but to stiffness. Follow the system through and you will soon find the cause.

Toning

The quality of a piano's tone is determined before it leaves the factory. Matters such as design and scaling, hammer strike points, the soundboard, action, strings and the general quality of the materials used determine the quality of tone. The more expensive a piano the better the quality and the tone. A new piano of a cheap range will understandably have tone of lesser quality. This also holds true when pianos get old: an old piano of fine quality will have a better tone, all other things being equal, than that of an old piano of cheap construction.

Piano tone cannot readily be classified, given numbers and filed into pigeon holes. It is a matter of individual taste. Some prefer a crisp, bright sound, others like it mellow. Next door

Figure 60. Tools and materials used in toning

neighbours may favour a quiet, soft tone. But nobody likes a piercing harsh sound, or its opposite, a confusing, mushy sound.

Factors leading to the gradual deterioration of tone quality as a piano gets older are: a flattened soundboard; rusting and tired strings; a worn-out action and mis-shapen, worn and packed, hard hammers. Putting all this to rights by replacing with new parts would involve enormous expenditure. But an improvement of some sort by revitalizing the hammers is possible and costs next to nothing. This chapter deals with getting the best possible sound out of what is left of old hammers.

Note: Toning cannot be carried out properly if the piano is badly out of regulation and badly out of tune. The action should be free and the unisons, at least, should be tuned smooth.

The tools which will be used: sandpaper strips; a sanding block; toning needles and holder; a wood chisel (*see* Figure 60).

Figure 61. A hammer in reasonable condition

UPRIGHT PIANOS

Figure 61 shows a hammer from the central region of the action, in reasonable condition and showing moderate wear. The three grooves caused by the strings will have packed hard and gathered dirt or rust, creating a hard sound. When filing a hammer, the aim is to restore it to its original, oval shape but at the same time to remove as little felt as possible. The hammers in the deep bass, because of their bulk, and lesser use, are often not in need of attention. Those in the high treble do not have much substance to them anyway, and filing may take the felt down to the wood.

1. Select three adjacent notes which you consider to be quite hard in sound.

2. Mark the tail of the middle hammer with a pencil, this hammer being used as a trial.

3. Remove the action and place it securely on a bench. If it is of the overdamped type then work may be easier if the damper system is removed and placed to one side.

4. Wrap a strip of sandpaper around the sanding block and hold the hammer firmly with your other hand. Starting at the tail-end of the shoulders, gently file the hammer with clean, straight strokes following the contours towards the indentations but not actually touching the crown, (*see* Figure 62). File the top and underside equally in turn, removing as little felt as possible, until the indentations are gradually eliminated. Do not file in the reverse direction or rub back and fore. Filing in a straight line will ensure that the hammer remains square in its thickness at the crown and, therefore, that it will be able to make even contact with the three strings.

Figure 62. Filing a hammer

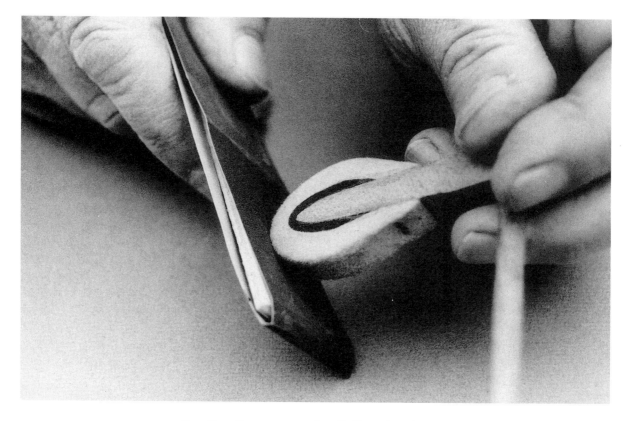

5. Gently remove the fluff at the tip of the hammer.

6. Replace the action and compare the tone of the trial hammer with those on either side. If there is a satisfactory improvement then continue with the others.

Needling

If a hard tone still persists after filing then the cause lies deeper: the felt in the interior of the hammer has been compacted through many years of playing and its resilience lost. The object of needling is to soften these inner parts, scratching on the surface will have no effect whatsoever.

1. Choose and mark a hammer for a practice run as for filing, remove the action and place it securely on a bench.

2. Remove the hammer section from the action. (Needling can be carried out with the hammer still installed in the action but the section will need to be held very firmly to avoid breaking the shank, as considerable force is needed to drive in the needles.)

3. Rest the hammer on a block, or at the edge of the bench, and needle through the shoulders only, never at the crown. If you imagine a hammer to be a wheel with a hub at the centre then the points of entry and direction of travel of the needles would be like spokes, several through each shoulder (*see* Figure 63).

Figure 63. Needling a hammer

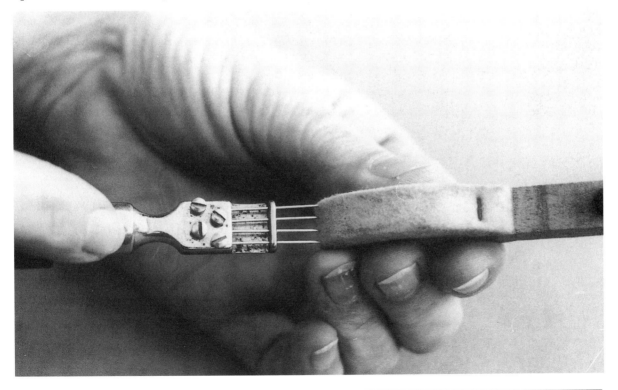

Ironing (1)

A piano tone which is too soft and muffled can be brightened by applying a hot iron to the hammers, provided they are in a reasonable condition. The ironing can be done with a broken wood chisel (being shorter will allow for better control) about twice the width of the hammer. Any similar tool with a flat surface will do but you need a handle because of the heat. The object is to compact and harden the hammer a little.

So that you do not commit 85 glorious mishaps select a hammer for a trial run and remove it from the action. Heat the end of the tool over a flame to about the heat of a domestic clothes iron on its medium setting, cover the hammer with wet cloth and place the iron on the tail end of the shoulders. Do not use a filing stroke as when using the sanding block but press firmly and roll the iron over the contours towards the crown, stopping before reaching the tip. Do both sides equally. Scorch marks are inevitable and can be easily removed by sanding.

Ironing (2)

A hammer which looks like a boiled egg with the top off is hardly worth bothering with but some improvement can be made. The flattened surface and deep indentations will cause it to cling to the strings, halting a clean rebound and creating a truly ugly sound. Foolishly filing away at the flattened crown simply to remove the grooves will add even further to the already considerable loss of felt and hammer length, resulting in an even worse sound (if that is possible.) A hammer's travel, because it pivots on a fixed centre, describes the arc of a circle. The more the hammer is shortened, the lower will be its point of strike on the strings and the higher up the shoulder will be its point of contact; further tonal problems, related to harmonics, will be the result.

This is a do-or-die operation. Heat the iron, cover the hammer with a wet cloth, lay the iron on the shoulders and press firmly, pulling and coaxing the felt towards the crown, thus trying to re-shape the hammer by re-distributing the felt.

GRAND PIANOS

Follow the instructions as given above for the upright. To save time the action need not be drawn fully out from the piano. Draw out just enough so as to have easy access to the hammers, leaving the back edge of the action resting on the keybed, and supporting the front end on a table.

Casework renovation

The methods of casework renovation as described here cost little, are within the capabilities of everyone and are good enough to bring a smile to the face of the most miserable looking piano. Owners of good quality instruments are advised either to study furniture repair and restoration more deeply, or seek expert attention and pay the price accordingly.

Impatience is the handyman's biggest downfall. Slapping on a final finish to an ill-prepared surface is a waste of time and money. Do all the groundwork first, i.e. 'making good' and 'surface preparation'. Leave the finishing until last.

UPRIGHT PIANOS

Making good

Bottom panel

Top panels are seldom missing but bottom panels frequently are.

1. Measure for size, and purchase a firm sheet of board about 6mm ($\frac{1}{4}$in.) thick. You will also need sufficient batten 75 × 20mm (3 × $\frac{3}{4}$in.), to fix to the inside edges of the board for reinforcement.

2. Drill through the panel, countersink and fix to the battens with screws long enough for a good fixing but that do not protrude through the other side.

3. Make good the countersunk holes with wood filler.

4. A panel has to be secured, top and bottom, to stop it from falling in and from falling out. The base of the panel is usually fixed by two stub dowels. Check for two holes in the wooden rail where the pedals are. If this is the case then hold the panel in position and mark for the dowels (an alternative method is given below, should there be no holes).

5. Measure the diameter of the dowel holes and obtain a short piece of suitable dowelling.

6. Drill holes (of the same diameter as the dowels in the batten at the bottom of the panel) where the marks have been made and glue in the dowels, leaving about 12mm ($\frac{1}{2}$in.) extending.

An alternative, and easier method, whether there are holes or not, is to fit two blocks to the bottom board of the piano, to stop the panel from falling in, and two tongues to the bottom batten of the panel to stop it from falling out.

Several arrangements using wooden swivel catches are used at the top of the panel allowing it to be easily removed yet kept securely in place when fitted. Study the layout for a few moments and see if anything remains of the original fixings.

Mouldings

To replace a section of missing or damaged moulding of the kind found around the edges of the top lid, make a cardboard template of the moulding contours. Grind down a piece of broken hacksaw blade to match the shape of the template, fit the shaped blade into a slotted wooden stock, select a suitable length of hardwood and then merrily scrape away for a year and a day. Not many have the facilities or the skill to do this and it will be hard to find enthusiasm for such a task if the piano is in such a weak condition that it ought to be put down humanely. But, what a relief, there is an alternative method.

1. If a good match cannot be found for the missing piece then remove *all* the remaining lengths of mouldings. Clean away the old glue from the sides of the lid and the fixed back section.

2. Purchase sufficient half-round moulding of the type used for general household purposes. The contours need not be the same as the original but it helps if the width is near the mark. If it is too wide then plane it down to size.

3. Cut the moulding to length, remembering that the corners must come together as mitre joints (i.e. at 45°).

4. Glue into place.

5. If you wish to boast of your 'solid as a rock' gluing technique then quietly drive home a few panel pins.

Damaged veneer

The usual area where damaged veneer is to be found is at the bottom of the side panels.

1. Pencil in a perfect right-angled section around the damage and, using a tenon saw where possible, or a chisel if not, cut at the pencil marks only to the depth of the veneer.

2. Carefully remove any pieces of veneer within the section using a wide-blade tool such as a paint scraper. Try not to dig into the main carcase.

3. Select a new piece of veneer of similar colour and grain. If the new piece is too thick then sand the underside. If too thin glue two pieces together.

4. Chamfer the edges of the cut-away section so that they bank down at an angle.

5. Cut the new piece of veneer just oversize and, for a perfect fit, chamfer the underside edges ready to interlock into position. After a few fittings and sandings it will slot into place and be ready for gluing.

Blistered veneer

Small blisters can sometimes be dealt with by using a hot clothes iron and a damp cloth. Place the damp cloth over the blister and press down with the hot iron. Tilt the iron so that only the affected part is treated. Re-soak the cloth now and again. The idea is to melt and re-distribute the caked-up glue. If this does not work then use a sharp knife and make an incision down the centre of the blister, following the grain. Scrape away any hard lumps of old glue and blow out the dust. Run in some fresh glue and clamp.

Risen veneer

If a large section of veneer has risen up at the edge of a panel clean out the old, dried glue, blow out the dust, sand if possible and re-glue. If cleaning is difficult use a sharp knife and a straight edge, and cut a flap large enough to be lifted up so as to allow work to be carried out underneath. Any hard lumps or dust left behind will make re-fixing difficult if not impossible.

A terrible veneer problem

A piano that has spent many years in extremely damp conditions, such as are often found in an underground room of a church, may have such dreadful veneer problems that a repair using new veneer would be very costly and in cases such as this not worthwhile anyway. Not to worry . . . such a piano can soon be made beautiful again for next to nothing.

1. Remove *all* the veneer from the worst affected panels. The loose pieces can be pulled away easily but some patches may prove to be stubborn. It may be necessary to use an electrical sanding appliance to remove difficult bits.

2. Finish by hand using a medium or coarse-grain paper wrapped around a block to smooth out the machine marks.

3. Using a fine-grade paper wrapped around a block, and following the grain in the wood, sand the whole surface.

4. Stain and varnish (see pp. 126–30) and your piano will be in showroom condition.

You will be branded a heathen by purists of the woodworking trade for doing all this, but if the piano resembles a flood-damage insurance write-off then what is there to lose?

Gouges

Fill deep gouges with a proprietary wood filler. Mix sufficient filler with the stain to be used later and work in well with your fingers before applying. Press firmly into the gouge and smooth off with a knife.

Hollows and shallow indentations, often found on the curve of the fall, the keyslip and arms are difficult to fill because the filling tends to fall out. Sand over an area larger than the indentations, gradually smoothing them out so that they are hardly noticeable.

Nicks are common on the fall lip (the part you take in your fingers when opening). Any fillings here will soon fall out. With a plane, take a skim along the whole length and round off the edge with sandpaper. This should not spoil its appearance or purpose.

Clamping

A re-glued section on top of the piano can be clamped by covering with a protective cloth and then placing a heavy weight on top. Leave for a day or two to dry. Should the repair be on the side of the piano then protect the area with a cloth, place a flat piece of board against the cloth and wedge a length of batten between the piano and a wall.

Castors

A piano has a high centre of gravity and can easily topple over. Broken or missing castors will aggravate this situation. A piano that is difficult to move because of its castors is not only dangerous to people but damaging to the floor.

The piano will need to be put on its back, and as even a small

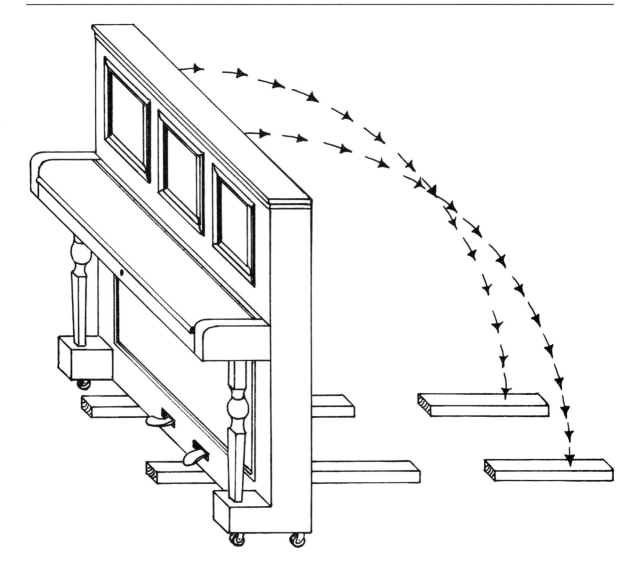

piano is heavy, get plenty of help. When lifting a piano bend your knees, keep your back and arms straight and lift by straightening your knees. Lift on to planks as shown in Figure 64. The piano can now be lowered on to its back without your fingers getting trapped, and the added height afforded by the planks will allow extra room for fixing the rear castors. (If the piano has moulding which extends over the back end of the fixed top lid then do not rest this on the planks.) After the new castors have been fitted the piano can now be uprighted on to the planks and set down squarely on the floor, with another pair of hands removing the planks. If you upright the piano without first lifting it on planks you will place a strain on the rear castors.

If your piano had done duty in places of public entertainment

Figure 64. A piano ready to be put on its back

then during its history its travels may have necessitated several changes of castors, of various shapes and sizes, leaving poor fixing potential because of the chewed-up wood. Use a wood chisel to even up the damaged area, and plug the holes. To bring into line, cut and fix a hardwood plate. A castor must have a good fixing in each of its plate holes. A screw which continues to go round when fully home is not a good fixing.

If you decide that new castors are not justified but you still wish to make the piano safe, then screw on two wooden runners, with shiny bottoms, from back to front, like a pair of skis, the runners being deep enough to regain the former pedal height. Whatever you do, never pack a piano up with blocks and books and bits of this and pieces of that.

Backing cloth

This is in the forgotten region of the piano. A dustproof cover at the back of a piano is as important for its well-being as the panels at the front. A torn backing cloth will allow dust and insects to settle on the back of the soundboard and ribs. Fitting a cloth costs next to nothing and is a simple operation.

1. Gently coax away the battens which hold the cloth in position. If removed intact then they can be used again. If they are dry and very brittle and you cannot help but break them, then any new batten to be used should be stained to a dark colour and allowed to dry before re-attaching.

2. A lifting bar is usually fitted midway across the back of the piano; unscrew this.

3. Remove all traces of the old cloth and scrape the rebates clean. Clean the back of the soundboard and ribs and clean out the bottom of the piano which is now accessible. Brush and vacuum away the debris then use a damp cloth, and dry off immediately afterwards.

4. Purchase a piece of any cheap, thin nylon or cotton material and cut to just oversize. (Too thick a material will reduce the volume of sound.)

5. Fix the material to the top rebate, pressing home a few drawing pins, and leave a little excess showing above the top. Fix the top batten with panel pins.

6. Using a few drawing pins fix the material to the two side rebates, gently pulling out sideways and downwards so you do not have any creases. Fit the two side battens.

7. When you are satisfied that the cloth is firm and without creases fit the bottom batten.

8. Before you replace the lifting bar pierce holes in the cloth where the screws enter, to prevent the screws from pinching and twisting the cloth.

9. Finally, trim around the edges with a razor blade.

You now have a neat, dustproof and vermin-proof protective cover at the back of your piano, which will be the envy of the street.

Surface preparation

Stripping

A finished surface is only as good as its preparation. Machines, blow lamps and manual scraping, unless expertly carried out, will leave the bare surface in a sorry state which will show through the final finish. Chemical stripping is a dirty, messy business, but it is quick and thorough and if properly carried out will not harm bare wood. Good planning before the job is started will allow you to slap on and splash about freely, without causing injury or damage. Worrying about bits flying here and there will not help at all.

The work is best done in a garage or outside. If it is inconvenient to move the piano then at least take the panels and fall outside. If the work has to be done inside the house then cover the floor and furniture in the room with newspapers and old sheets, leaving the windows open for ventilation. Have a bowl of water and a cloth at the ready to wash off any chemical which might get on your skin. Remove the action and keys, and drape and pin old sheets over the keybed, strings, pedal trapwork and backing cloth. Wear rubber gloves, protective goggles and old clothes, and keep your arms well covered.

Using a large, soft paintbrush, lay the stripper on thick and do not agitate or brush it out. Let the chemical do the work. Leave for 20 minutes or so, until the surface has bubbled up and then work off with wire wool. A further application will probably be necessary as there will always be stubborn areas here and there. Do not neglect mouldings and crevices and use an old toothbrush for getting into awkward corners. Clean away any remaining sludge with a rag, especially remembering the back of the keyslip and between the hinges on the fall and the top lid.

You now need to neutralize the chemically treated surface. Wash it clean with soap and water then give it a final rinse with clean water. Do not leave any puddles lying about and hasten the drying-off with a cloth.

The surface will now need sanding. Using a fine-grade sandpaper, wrapped around a block for large flat surfaces, sand lightly with the grain until you obtain a smooth surface, then dust off the surface.

Staining

The next step is to stain the wood to the desired colour. A small tin of stain is sufficient to cover a piano. The colour will be indicated on the tin and instructions given. Application is easy and in most cases, one coat, evenly applied with a fluff-free, dry cloth, is enough. If you want to re-finish the piano in a much lighter colour than the original, going from black to light brown for example, then the stripped casework will need to be bleached before you apply the stain.

Make up about a six-pint solution of five parts water to one part household bleach and brush on evenly, covering every part of the surface. Quite dark patches may need a further application. Leave to dry then neutralize with clean water. Leave to dry again and lightly sand before staining. After staining do not sand the wood but wipe clean with a dry cloth.

Re-finishing

Varnishing

Varnishing should be carried out in a dust-free room at normal temperatures. Do not use old, worn-out paintbrushes but a previously used brush, if thoroughly clean and in good condition, is best, as it will have lost its splayed-out appearance and developed a compact, angled, working edge. If there are no suitable used brushes to hand then buy new ones: one of medium size and one small.

Semi-gloss polyurethane is the popular finish of today and is easier to apply than full gloss. Stir the contents of the tin well with a clean, thin strip of wood. Feel around the bottom of the tin for any thick deposits, break them up with the stick and stir them in. This will distribute the pigments evenly and ensure that the varnish is full-bodied when applied.

Dip the brushes into the varnish and work them out (as if painting) on a piece of clean scrapwood, spreading the varnish well into the bristles and shedding any loose hairs, which can then be picked off.

The art of any painting project is an even, well-brushed-in, well-layed-off application, on a well-prepared surface using clean brushes. 'Runs', the trademark of the amateur painter, are caused by an uneven and unworked slapping-on of finish, and by turpentine substitute being left in the brushes.

Several thin coats, each lightly sanded when dry, are better than one thick coat.

Varnishing a plain, bottom panel

Large surfaces are best tackled by breaking them up into imaginary sections. Lay the panel on a table and judge about a third of the length and a third of the width. You now have nine imaginary rectangular sections as shown in Figure 65.

It is now a case of 'painting by numbers'.

Figure 65. 'Painting by numbers', plain panel

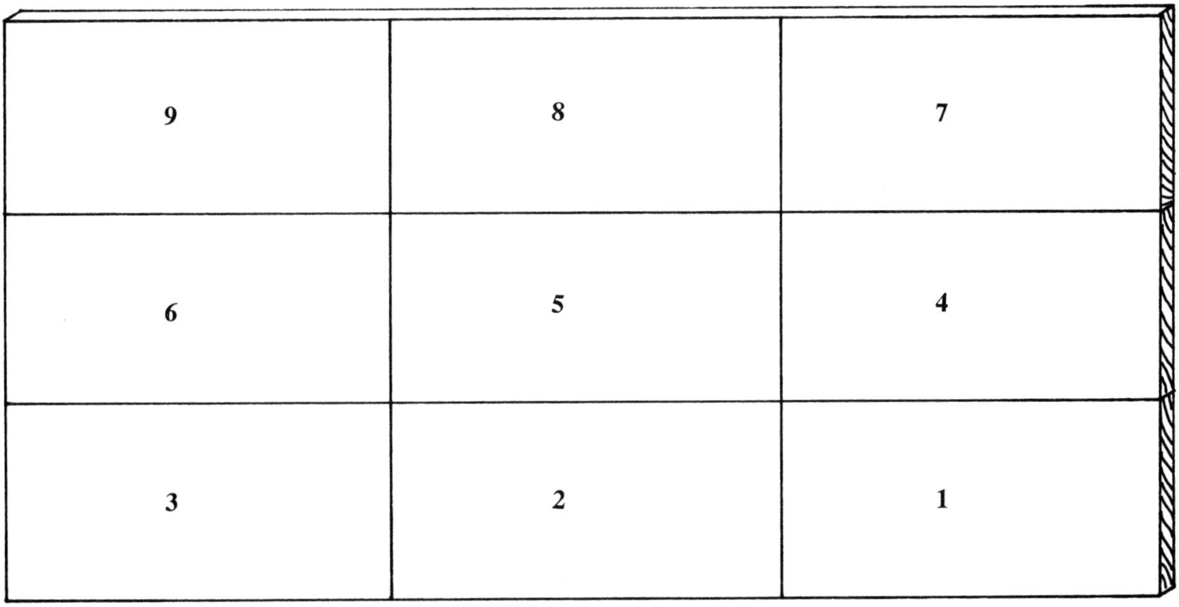

1. Using the larger brush, apply varnish to **(1)**. Work in well and brush out in all directions for a complete and even coverage. Recharge the brush when it begins to drag, wiping off any excess on the inside of the rim. If the brush slides too freely then the coat is too thick and you should thin out by brushing into **(2)**. When the varnish has been worked in well, lay off with firm, straight, even strokes, starting at the corner of **(1)** moving down the edge of the panel as far as **(2)** and then back in the opposite direction, just slightly overlapping the first run. Continue with these straight, even strokes until you have just reached **(4)**. Keep the brush moving, do not raise until the end of a run and do not start a movement in the middle of the surface. Lay off again using light strokes only.

2. Apply varnish to **(2)**. Work in well and brush back slightly into **(1)**. Brush off any excess into **(3)**. When satisfied that you have an even, complete coverage lay off with firm, straight, even strokes through **(1)** and **(2)** overlapping each time, then lay off again with light pressure. Occasionally, look at your work from all angles and correct any thin or thick spots by brushing out and laying off again. Work quickly as there is still a long way to go.

3. Apply varnish to **(3)**, work in well and brush back slightly into **(2)**. Lay off, first with firm pressure then with light pressure, working all the way through **(1)**, **(2)** and **(3)**. Using the small brush, clean off any dribbles which may have run over the edge.

4. Move quickly to **(4)**, working in and brushing out well, but this time just encroaching into **(1)**. Lay off this section as before, paying special attention to the 'join' between **(1)** and **(4)**.

5. Apply varnish to **(5)**, working in well, brushing back into **(4)**, and sideways, just into **(2)**. Brush out any excess into **(6)**. Lay off through **(4)** and **(5)**, remembering the 'join'.

6. Work on **(6)**. brushing back into **(5)** and **(3)** and lay off completely through **(4)**, **(5)** and **(6)**, remembering to smooth out the join.

The routine is now clear. Complete **(7)**, **(8)** and **(9)** in the same manner. If you have worked quickly then all the varnish will still be workable. For that final touch of finesse lay off the whole surface with a fairly dry brush and very light strokes and for that final dash of panache use the small brush, and deft strokes of the wrist to clean up the edges. Watch the work for a while and brush out any signs of runs.

Leave until thoroughly dry (two or three days in damp weather), sand lightly with the grain, dust off and repeat the whole process two or three times.

Varnishing a top panel with moulded sections

This is the most conspicuous part of the piano, so you do not want runs, bald patches and brush marks. Paint 'by numbers' as shown in Figure 66.

1. Using the small brush, not heavily charged, paint the mouldings **(1)**. Brushing in all directions is not easy on these long, narrow strips, but work the varnish in as well as you can. Remove any excess varnish from the brush on the rim of the tin and lay off. Pay attention to the corners and brush out any bubbles. The brush should feel reasonably dry when laying off mouldings.

Figure 66. 'Painting by numbers', panel with mouldings

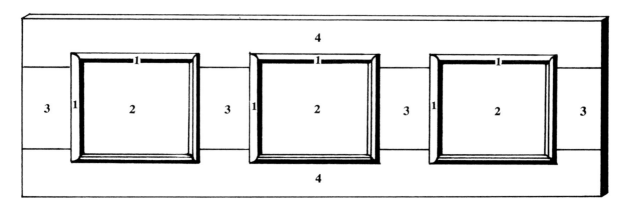

2. Using the large brush, apply varnish to the sections marked (2), work in well and lay off from side to side with the grain. Without re-charging, use the small brush and lay off the inside edges of the mouldings, brushing out any excess varnish which may accumulate in the corners.

3. Using the small brush, varnish the upright sections (3), brush in well and lay off. Wipe off any excess varnish from the brush on the rim of the tin and clean away any visible dribbles.

4. Apply varnish to the top and bottom (4), using the small brush: work well in, lay off with full sweeps and clean up the edges.

5. Watch the work until it settles and spread out any sign of a dribble. Leave to dry, sand, and repeat two or three times.

Varnishing the remaining parts

1. Fallboard
The fallboard will need to be done in two stages—open and closed. Place it on a work table and put in the open position. Work using three imaginary sections (divided lengthways only this time), brushing well in and well out and finally laying off completely along the length. Watch particularly the underside of the curve for runs. Keep a small cloth handy, slightly damped with turpentine substitute, in order to clean the brass hinge. When thoroughly dry put into the closed position and varnish, again using imaginary sections. Brush away any dribbles from

the sides or the fall may not close properly when re-fitted.

2. Top lid

Similarly, the top lid will need to be done in two stages. Be sparing with the application on the mouldings and brush out any sign of runs. Ensure that the pins and strings are well protected.

3. Side panels

'Painting by numbers' is again the best approach for the sides. Be extra careful when painting on the vertical as little trickles may turn into waterfalls.

4. Small sections

Use the small brush only on small sections such as the legs and do not have it too wet. There will not be much opportunity for brushing out in all directions but the varnish must still be worked in and not simply layed off. Watch the edges and crevices for accumulation and brush out with a fairly dry brush.

Cleaning brushes

You cannot do too much in one session with one set of brushes. A brush in use for too long, or left idle, will soon become matted and unuseable. Clean brushes immediately after use as follows.

1. Put the brushes into a jar of turpentine substitute and swill around, pressing on the bottom of the jar, then wiping on the rim to remove excess fluid.

2. Wash the brushes in a bowl of hot water and washing powder.

3. Rinse under the cold-water tap.

4. Roll the brush handles vigorously between the hands to remove excess water and leave to dry before using again.

Cosmetic beauty treatment

For the sake of a few blemishes, a full strip, stain and re-finish is unnecessary. If your piano is in a good state of general health, has all its faculties but looks a little jaded—as if it could do with a fortnight in the sun—then an easy-to-do course of beauty treatment will soon cheer it up.

Small burns

Wrap a small piece of fine-grade sandpaper around the end of a pencil and sand the charred area. If, after removing the burnt outer skin, the colour is still dark, wrap a small piece of cloth around the end of the pencil, dip into household bleach and apply to the burn. Allow time for the bleach to work then wipe with a damp cloth.

White rings

These are caused by hot drinks being placed on top of the piano (take note). Put some cigarette ash into a little water and mix to a paste. Apply to the affected area with a cloth. Alternatively, an equal mixture of linseed oil and methylated spirits will remove the stain, but may soften the polish and dull the appearance.

Emulsion stains

A damp cloth and gentle persuasion will soon get rid of these.

Paint speckles

Sanding will leave the piano in a worse state than if left alone. Pick off specks of paint with the fingernails.

Proprietary cosmetic products

Various products such as stain removers, scratch fillers, revivers, restorers, oils and waxes are on the market. Follow the maker's instructions and they will put new life into a lacklustre casework. Each tin, bottle or tube will contain more than you need initially but there will always be something else around the house in need of perking-up.

French polishing

The basic principles of french polishing seem simple enough, but turning out fine quality work needs years of experience. The old craftsman would cast a knowing eye over the work to be done, assess the wood, choose the right mix of materials, feel the mood of the rubber and vary his technique of application as his eye and sense of touch directed. Today his skills are not used in the commercial production of furniture—and a small piece would cost a fortune because of the labour costs alone. Today's household effects pass down a production line and are machine sprayed.

A revival of the magnificent art of french polishing would be welcome and you are encouraged to delve further into the subject, as one day it may be the sole property of the amateur enthusiast.

What follows is but a summary, sufficient for you to make a start on your piano. Reasonable results can be expected from a learner who is prepared to have a go, but at your first attempt do not expect to arrive at the beautiful, deep shine as still seen on many old pianos which have been properly cared for.

It is worthwhile to practise on the most shabby and unimportant piece of furniture in the house (perhaps the piano itself is the obvious candidate). Work in a dust-free room at no less than normal temperature, cover the floor and give yourself plenty of room. You will need a work table, large enough to take the panels and high enough to work comfortably (it is a lengthy job). It is impossible to do a good job if the work moves about, so arrange a fixing system to keep the panels steady. A small table for materials must be at hand.

The materials you need are: pieces of non-fluffy white cotton (handkerchiefs are ideal but not new as the fibres will be stiff); non-medicated cotton wool (soft and not lumpy); fine-grade wire wool; linseed oil; methylated spirits; and a bottle of french polish. All these items are easily obtainable. **Warning**: Always use glass jars, as metal containers may cause a chemical reaction.

Getting started

Note: All the surfaces must be thoroughly prepared beforehand.

Take a piece of linen 20cm (8in.) square and place a wad of cotton wool in the centre. Pick up the folds of the linen and twist until pear shaped. This is what is known as the 'rubber'. Open the folds, pour a little polish on to the cotton wool, gently squeeze and re-fold. Press the rubber on to a folded sheet of sandpaper, smooth side up, until the polish percolates and is evenly distributed. The rubber should now be flattened and in the shape of half a pear (see Figure 67). Check that there are no wrinkles on the flattened underside of the rubber, as this is the part which is about to go to work on the wood.

For the purpose of this exercise the piece to be worked on is a plain bottom panel, firmly secured to the work table, sanded, stained and free of dust.

1.   With charged rubber at the ready, hover above one of the corners furthest away, ready to work longways with the grain. Descend on the edge of the panel, move in a long, straight sweep, keep the pressure on and do not lift until you reach the other end. Return the other way slightly overlapping the first run. Do not stop during the course of a run, even momentarily, as a mark will appear. Keep going from left to right, right to left, just slightly overlapping the previous run each time, until the whole surface has been covered. Should the rubber begin to drag re-charge with a little more polish and press down on the sandpaper for

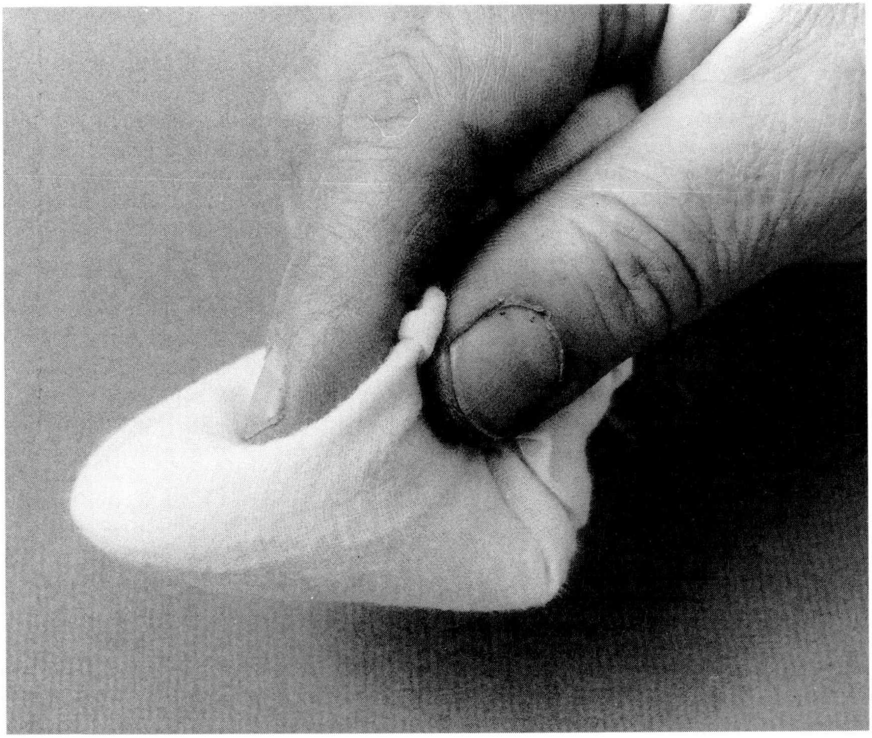

Figure 67. Making a 'rubber'

even distribution. Do not refuel in mid-air, but complete the run first. Check the bottom of the rubber occasionally and pull out any wrinkles. Repeat the process three or four times then leave to dry for a day or two. Do not expect to see a wonderful gloss just yet, though a hint of a shine should start showing. This stage acts as a sealer and a base for the next state.

2.   Using the finest grade wire wool and a very light touch rub down the whole surface, with the grain, and dust off with a clean, soft cloth. Your old rubber will now be useless unless it was kept in an airtight jar and it is better to make up a new one. Charge the rubber as before but this time add a few drops of linseed oil. To ensure that you do not use too much oil, pour a small quantity into a glass dish and apply to the rubber with your finger. Press down on the back of a piece of sandpaper so that the rubber takes on the shape of half a pear, and so that you distribute evenly the polish and oil. Check for wrinkles.

   Start at a far corner of the panel and, using circular polishing movements, gradually work along the sides and towards the centre. Work by first using small circles and then larger ones. Do not rush, just keep a steady rhythm going. When you feel the need to re-charge lift the rubber off quickly. Do not delay or the polish may begin to dry in patches and your work will be in vain. You can sometimes re-charge your rubber by pressing down on the sandpaper and taking up the surplus. The rubber, when freshly charged, will need only a light pressure but when it begins to drag increase the pressure and work a little further before re-charging. Continue polishing in circular motions, re-charging when necessary (remembering to apply only a finger-touch of oil) until the entire surface has been covered. Leave to dry thoroughly.

3.   Gently use the wire wool over the surface to remove any dust specks and key the surface and then wipe the surface clean. Repeat the process as in stage 2 but this time a few drops of linseed oil may be dropped here and there on to the panel. The rubber, during its circular polishing movements, will be given a 'glide' as it picks up the oil. You must understand that the purpose of the oil is to allow the rubber to polish freely; it is not a factor of the shine. Too much oil and the work will never dry. You will indeed get a 'wet' shine because of the oil but this is not the shine which is your ultimate aim—so do not get excited and rush out into the street singing when this happens. Use the oil sparingly. Do not hurry but take your time, covering the same patch well, with small then large circles, gradually covering new ground, the whole operation taking about 20 to 30 minutes. Allow to dry and gently use the wire wool. Repeat the whole process of stage 3 again . . . and again . . . and yet again, until a good 'body' has been built up.

4.   The final stage: check that the surface is completely free of dust. Charge the rubber with polish, assisting the distribution by pressing down on to the sandpaper then add *just a few drops* of methylated spirits, applied to the flattened pad with your finger. Use the rubber as in stage 1; long, straight, even sweeps from one end to the other, not lifting off until the end of the run and not re-starting in the middle of the surface. Work from left to right, right to left, slightly overlapping each time until the whole panel has been covered, keeping your fingers crossed for success.

The 'knowing eye' and the 'mood' of the rubber, can never be explained in words but such things eventually come to those who try hard enough.

Small sections

Use a rubber about half normal size. Small circles then larger ones are obviously inappropriate here but try to use some kind of polishing-in movement as well as laying off. Apply thinly, especially on narrow legs, as polishing on the vertical may result in runs.

Just a touch up

Your piano casework is in good condition, the original french polish sound and intact, but it looks a little dreary and in need of livening up. A full strip and re-finish is not necessary, just a 'touch up'. This is an ambitious project, highly skilled and it can go disastrously wrong. I would advise that you try it out on an inconspicuous section first, such as the underside of the top lid.

Gently rub down the surface with wire wool and wipe clean. Just prior to using the charged rubber wipe the surface with a soft cloth slightly damped with methylated spirits. This helps to soften the old polish, allowing it to mix with the new. Apply the rubber using straight, long sweeps from one end to the other and back again, slightly overlapping each time, and now, more than ever, do not raise the rubber until the end of a run nor re-start in the middle of the surface. Let the work dry out and the decision whether to continue with the rest of the piano is yours.

Brushing on

Imagine a yellow room in a country cottage: pine-strip floors; pine-panelled walls; pine tables and chairs; wickerwork baskets; rocking chairs; rush mats; and a wood-burning stove. A dirty, old, dark-brown piano will surely look out of place. Before chopping it up and feeding it to the stove consider the merits of brush-on polish—cheap, and relatively easy to apply compared with conventional polishing.

Chemically strip, sand and prepare the surfaces as already explained, but *do not apply stain*. Pour some french polish (a choice of hues is available) into a wide-necked jar and using two paintbrushes, one medium and one small, paint on the polish in the manner described in the section on varnishing (pp. 126–30). Many thin coats will be necessary; allow each one to dry thoroughly then gently rub down. Clean the brushes immediately after use with methylated spirits, then wash in hot water and soap, rinse in cold water, roll between the hands and allow to dry.

Who knows, your piano could be under threat from the axe one minute and transformed to pride of place the next!

The last waltz

Your piano has played its last tune. You look out of the window on a dismal, grey morning and watch the piano tuner walking away, head bowed, clutching his black bag. You had asked for a second opinion . . . and got it. He has just pronounced your piano as clinically dead.

You look lovingly at such a beautiful case and think. 'What a pity, isn't there something I can do?'

Well, there is.

1.   Remove and set aside, the panels and fall.

2.   Take out the keys and action and dispose of them.

3.   If the keybed can be unscrewed then remove it and put to one side. If there is no sign of any screws then it has been secured to the case with glued dowels so leave it where it is.

4.   Remove the two rails of key pins, the keybed base and dispose of them.

5.   Take out, and throw out, the horizontal and vertical rods, hinges and all the other pedal fitments, but keep the pedal feet and arms.

6.   Remove all fittings to which the action had been secured and dispose of them.

7.   Using the tuning lever, take the tension out of all the strings then cut them off and dispose of them carefully. It is dangerous to cut the strings without first easing the tension.

8.   Unscrew and dump the iron frame (it's heavy).

9.   Remove the soundboard and discard.

10.   Remove the tuning-pin plank. If this proves difficult then just take out the tuning pins and throw them away. The inside of the piano has now been stripped.

11.   Use a hacksaw to shorten the pedal arms, leaving just enough to be firmly screwed to the bottom board inside the piano, allowing the pedals to be seen as normal on the outside.

12.   Line the back of the piano where the soundboard and tuning plank had been with thin, but firm, board and screw into place.

13.   Line the tuning plank with thin board if not already removed.

14.   Re-fit the keybed (if removed). At the bottom of the keybed, where the original base was, fit a shelf extending back as far as the back lining which has just been fitted in place of the soundboard.

15. About halfway between the keybed and the top of the piano fix a shelf right across from one side to the other. Do not bring it flush to the front edges of the side panels but leave sufficient room for the top front panel to be replaced.

16. Fit the fall back into position and screw it down at the back corners so that it can be opened but not removed.

17. Put the top panel on a workbench and reinforce the inside edges if they are not of solid construction.

18. Line the inside of the top panel with worktop material as used in kitchens.

19. Cut two rebates at the bottom of the panel and fit two brass hinges.

20. Cut two corresponding rebates at the back of the fall, place the panel in position and screw together.

21. Fit two sliding stays, or brass chains, to the former position of the fixing clips on the back of the panel and the inside of the piano.

The top of the piano is now a drop-door drinks-dispensing cabinet.

22. Line what was the keybed with an attractive baize of velvet.

23. Using clear plastic strips, section this area off into small boxes.

24. You can add an attractive feature by installing a light that comes on when the fall is opened.

You now have a showcase for your proudest possessions and mementos, such as old coins (or parking tickets).

25. Fit a shelf to the bottom section, about halfway up.

26. Saw the bottom panel right down the centre into two equal halves.

27. Reinforce the inside edges of both halves if necessary.

28. Cut two rebates into the inside of the outside edges of each half and fit brass hinges to them.

29. Cut two corresponding rebates out of each side of the piano and screw in what are now double doors

30. Fit a small knob to each door.

31. Fit a magnetic, or ball-and-socket catch to keep the two doors together.

32. Fit a doorstop just inside the piano between the pedals.

33. Alternatively, you could fit the two halves as sliding doors, but avoid a drop-door—it won't do your shins any favours.

You now have a handy place for storing man-size bottles and glasses. You may feel a little sad at seeing your piano pensioned-off in such a fashion . . . but at least you will be able to drown your sorrows.

GRAND PIANOS

Stripping, re-finishing and allied tasks are the same as for the upright.

Loose top lid

This is a common problem. The strip of wood available on the rim, and the fixing potential of the hinges, are not generous when you consider the size, weight and angle of the lid when opened to maximum. Repair as follows.

1. Remove the lid and place it on a bench. If the hinges are twisted a new pair will be needed.

2. Cut away squarely any damaged areas of the rebates.

3. Pack the screw holes with hardwood plugs (*not* used matches) and make the rebates up to height (if need be) with hardwood veneer.

4. Glue, tack and allow to dry.

5. Sand flush to the side of the case.

6. Mark for the screw holes and start the holes.

7. Fit the hinges to the lid but do not screw home fully.

8. You will need assistance when fitting the lid to the piano. Screw in the hinges and check for correct fit before giving each screw a final turn.

Lifting a grand piano

You will need to raise the piano a little off the floor if the legs or castors need attention. Only one leg at a time need be raised. One or more volunteers will be required to lift and to slide a stout table underneath. If no help is at hand, place a low, strong table in position, and with a flat piece of wood held in position to protect the underside of the piano, lift with—you've guessed it—a car jack.

GRAND FINALE

Action like a sewing machine? . . . Nicely in tune? . . . Everthing shining? . . . Then you'll enjoy the next part . . .

1. Open the fall.

2. Place your music on the stand.

3. Put your stool in position.

4. Now sit down and play and help make the world go round.

The End

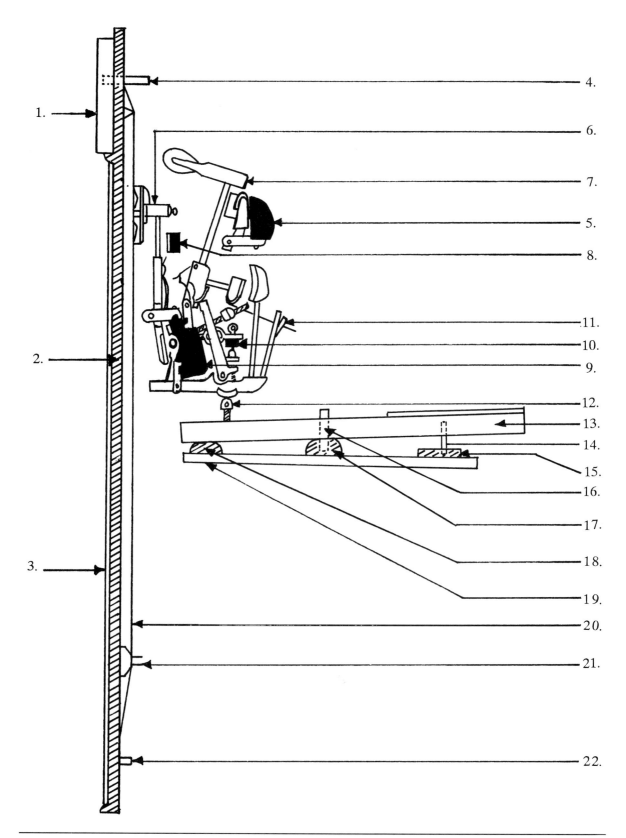

The parts of the piano

Figure 68. The parts of the piano

Key

1 pin block
2 iron frame
3 soundboard
4 tuning pin
5 hammer-rest rail
6 damper section
7 hammer section
8 damper-spring rail
9 main action rail
10 button rail
11 lever section
12 key capstan
13 key
14 front-rail pin
15 front rail
16 balance-rail pin
17 balance rail
18 back rail
19 key bed
20 string
21 bridge pins
22 hitch pin

Suppliers

H.J. Fletcher and Newman Ltd
Unit 10A Dartford Trade Park
Powder Mill Lane
Dartford
Kent DA1 1QB

Telephone: 0322 26441/2/3

Heckscher and Company
75 Bayham Street
London NW1 0AA

Telephone: 071 387 1735/6888

Index

Figures in bold indicate Figure nos